The Unusual Path To Success

How to create wealth anywhere in the world

By

Ralton M. Thompson

DEDICATION

This book is for anyone who has ever been abandon, robbed, scammed, failed at anything, or was ever called a loser, and for all my children who will learn the hard way in life if they don't follow my instructions.

AUTHOR'S NOTE

The Unusual Path to Success is a different book experience which covers a prodigious amount of self-improvement tips and wealth building habits that avowedly ties into many principles from the Holy bible. One of the core concepts in this book is to focus on small improvements and watch it impact your life daily.

The book explains how many people struggle in various areas of life because they lack access to wealthy information. The author also brings out how small businesses and entrepreneurs stay in one position and never grow, comparing good business practices against bad ones with his research and studies.

If you're looking for a book to give you a better understanding of how your mindset affects your self-worth, your goals, and your view on the world, then you have found it. There are so many limitations and financial traps setup to push people into a trajectory not intended for good. And the author presents many lessons on how you can navigate through these struggles, when you become a corporate leader, a business owner, or even a celebrity. The Unusual Path to Success contains a lot of real-world exit strategies we need, so that makes it very fascinating read and everyone who reads this book will discover their true path to success.

PREFACE

The High-Value Purpose

My whole mission over the years has been dedicated in a creating one book that would encompass a little bit of everything in one place. And while I was writing *The Unusual Path to Success*, I began turbocharging the systems and strategies I mentioned in the book. So, for every reader who will own a copy, you will have the best practical knowledge on how to respond to any challenging situation on your directed path.

The principal intention is to take everyone on a journey through self-discovery, mental wellness, and a path to transformation. Not only that, but to provide a helpful guide that encourages business interest and soul-searching in others. I used my own life experiences to show all the step-by-step circumstances I underwent using diverse examples. And I was willing to be truthful and unguarded so I can build a relatable connection with my audience. This advantage will give every reader a front row seat to their own story after understanding their purpose.

TABLE OF CONTENTS

ACKNOWLEDGEMENT

This ensemble of work is credited to the financial hardship many of us face today. So, I am expressively indebted to *God* for correcting me on this "path to success" cause only He was able to show me all the humbling experiences I could wish for. I realized writing a book was a lot more challenging than I ever thought, yet I still didn't give up. Because I knew it would bring forth innumerable rewards I couldn't even imagined. To my mentors and teachers who have been supportive throughout my career and to those who have worked sincerely hard in providing me with the necessary tools and information, I thank you.

But my true superstars are the ones who will read this book and I am forever grateful that I could share this evocative wealth of knowledge I have gathered over time, in hopes you can find prosperity and become great anywhere on this planet. I had the pleasure of working with some amazing individuals, business partners, staff members and people who have helped me in many field projects; to everyone out there, I am truly thankful as well.

I could never leave out the members of my family, from siblings to nieces, nephews, and cousins. Everyone has helped with my personal guidance and the appreciation for many things, so don't think I will ever forget anyone. I will say, no other human has had more instrumental push for this project than the man himself, Dr. Myles Munroe, who dedicated his ministry and research in the transforming people like me and many others to pursue *God* and staying on their spiritual journey.

To the adopted mothers and fathers, I have everywhere, my blessings are with you; all of you have never stopped providing your unremitting love and lectures, and all those inspirational advices I got when I needed it.

But none of this recognition wouldn't be arrant, if I didn't have great friends that all waited patiently before they could see one line from this book. The list is so much the name right now but thank you for understanding why I was very distant for months at a time, all those late nights I was up working and writing, it all paid off.

In the end my mother's fundamental teachings stood by me, for every single struggle, accomplishment, and success that I ever experience, her words helped me. For her there is no amount of thank you or gifts that would ever express a son's love, I will miss her forever, Mrs. Winnifred "Monica" Thompson. In addition to that, *God* please bless everyone's heartbeat out there, and let them enjoy this book.

INTRODUCTION

"Every success story always starts with a small beginning..."
— ***Ralton Thompson*** *(Author, entrepreneur)*

This book will be an investment to learn powerful strategies, mind-revealing content and life lessons to improve yourself, your relationships, and your character to operate in any business or industry of your choice. For generations only a small amount of people has ever amassed wealth through families or inheritance, but with this book you can change that.

When I was growing up, I had big dreams and visions of success at an early age. I remember the struggles in my childhood stages, then being a teenager and now an adult. And I realize that my dreams and aspirations to become successful didn't come easy. Because I wanted to be known for my exceptional skills and gifts that came with me. I just needed the guidance, discipline, and mentorship to develop myself and my brand.

So, the big questions are: What will be your success story? And what or who will be behind your success? I'll be honest no one truly cares until they have heard about you, and that is a harsh truth. A lot of people will tell you what you want to hear, but this book is not about that, I did not make up anything to win over the hearts and spirits of people to sell them a dream. Because to me, demonstration is more important than memorization. And we should function in the way as educated people, not what is recited or memorize from a test, a music video, or an experiment.

There are a lot of self-help books out there that can give you a great deal of information, but to what end? The biggest part of my success came from learning and reading other people's work. But it was when I put everything that I've read and understood into action that's when things started to turn around.

> *"There are no secrets to success. It is the result of preparation, hard work, and learning from failure."* — **Colin Powell** *(Former U.S. Secretary of State)*

Because we are living in different times today, different circumstances will always appear in our lives to test us or to destroy us. And everyone knows most days can be more difficult than others, even when you have everything you need. There is an important challenge you will always face when it comes to personal development, because we have everything in this world and at our fingertips to distract us daily. When you become self-aware of how your thoughts and attitudes affect your life, you can then choose to expand your mindset. A lot of individuals think it's normal to inspirit the notion "we must fake it until we make it" and that is not the right state of mind to be in. My self-confidence grew when I understood what I wanted most out of life and finding my purpose. I believe if we fake it or pretend to do things that we are not happy about. It sometimes leads to depression and lessens new possibilities to create opportunities you would encounter if you're in the wrong place or in the wrong field. In order to cope with difficult situations or with any setbacks you are facing today, you need to build up a variety of different techniques and tools to manage them well.

How can I stay motivated?

Have you always wondered how you could increase your motivation to complete something? Well, there are many ways of increasing your motivational drive, but the most important thing to understand about motivation is that it's never steady, some days you got it, and other days you don't. It changes from situation to situation and from person to person because we know everyone is different. The best thing is to be aware of what really motivates you in achieving that desired goal. I'll be honest I was truly excited about writing this book and getting it published sooner than expected, but there were delays and bad negotiations, I just didn't feel like writing or going out to meet with people. But I started to reflect on why I was doing it in the first place and then I pinpointed the value it would bring to my audience and my readers.

The main ingredient behind everything we see or have in our possession is *value,* and what you value the most, is what you naturally end up going after. So, if value money, you'll go after money and if you value fame, you'll go after fame and the list goes on. When looking to advance your success it will demand many things from you on a regular basis, but your willpower and your determination comes at the top of the list. Many people believe that we are born with the determination and those who succeed are simply the fortunate ones who got it in abundance. Yet if you ask any successful individual, they will tell you they struggled with many drawbacks including staying motivated. However, they always found a way to channel and use what they had more effectively. So, use this book with all the shared knowledge and experience in it, that it may enrich your life in many ways.

Chapter 1

The Preparation Process

"To be prepared is half the victory..."
— **Miguel de Cervantes** Saavedra (Spanish writer)

First, I want to congratulate you in acquiring this book; the next challenge is to complete it. I have learnt that the best places to find great ideas are in books. Many of us read so we know we're not alone, either with our struggles or with our achievements. To understand why we are here, we must first acknowledge we were chosen; yes, we don't always pick our purpose in life, sometimes it choses us.

I know many people have a desire to shift their lives and make the necessary changes to be more productive and resourceful in the years to come. So, try not to waste any time that you cannot get back. For this reason, I implore you to spend each moment developing yourself and learning new skills in going forward. You might be an employee looking to escape the 9-5 life, a freelancer, a student, maybe even an entrepreneur or business owner seeking solace from a dying business and want to be more successful than how you are today, whatever it is you do, the key to a better future starts with you.

The decisions you make going forward, will affect every outcome that as not arrived yet. DO NOT OVERTHINK what you are thinking now. Try to learn from it and understand it. Our current situations or things from our past are not always our faults; it's an effect from someone else's miseducation, greed, selfishness, destructive behavior, poor means of preparedness and most of all, lack of training.

Think back and see where you have gone wrong or where you've been misled. In today's world, everyone is trying to get rich or wealthy overnight, and there is this survival of the fittest mentally that goes with it. *But there's no quick way in creating or building a wealth, your craft or any multiple streams of income in one night or one week,* even if you win the lottery, you first must be reprogrammed, retrained, and be redeem from all the systems that are in place which already hold you back. **The preparation for the marathon must first be accepted in your heart (mind) not in your eyes.**

"There are no shortcuts to any place worth going" —**Beverly Sill**
(American operatic singer)

To get what you want out this life or to become everything you desire, a lot of demands must be met, and much will have to be sacrificed. This many of us already know BECAUSE NOTHING WORTH HAVING WILL EVER COME EASY.

I am so grateful *God* blessed me with a mother that had an esurient desire for knowledge and for me to learn more. Over the years this desire grew daily, and from it I started teaching others how to attain great personal success. But I spent years building and growing my knowledge and my influence which took longer than I planned, because I was misinformed in school, lacking the right resources to get ahead, and suffered through memory retention. Without much avail, I was swimming in a lot of personal debt up until my early 30's. Even with all the jobs I had in Sales, Construction, Agriculture and in Banking, I was still nowhere where I wanted to be. So, in December of 2015, I decided not to be in the rat race for the millions and I quit my job at Wells Fargo Bank in Wyoming and moved to New York.

2

I began learning all I could about financial literacy plus all the successful habits why the rich don't work for money, I started watching videos, but I was still not getting rich. But then I did something different, I went into business for myself as an *independent contractor,* so I could secure contracts with companies like JetBlue Airways, Delta Airlines, NAPA Auto Parts, Advance Auto, and a few other private companies. They all needed Distribution services, and I was already in the transportation industry to expand my services, so it was like **preparation meets opportunity**.

Before my journey there, I used to live on the beautiful island of Jamaica. Yes, this is the place with the white sandy beaches, great food, and the world-renowned Reggae music, but sadly our job opportunities are limited there, and the natural resources are always being exploited overseas to make billions. Now I had to sacrifice all that and more to be here in America and experience the trials and hardship that came with it.

I failed so many times I knew I had to learn new skills to get ahead, so I started to adjust my attitude and my mindset, this made me realize that anything and everything is humanly possible with *God,* ONLY if we *trust the process*. To speak on a great influence that guided me, my mother was a lady of such rarity and standard even in our home country she held high esteem, but unfortunately, she passed away in February of 2020.

My greatest wish was to have her here with me today and to see the success of this book. Knowing that she had taught me so many life lessons and proverbs to live by. It was the privilege she gave me to travel so early and experience so much at a tender age, that helped me understood what it takes to make it into a foreign land. I saw my future before I started it, so I developed a passion for reading, the languages, history, and the arts, unfortunately my qualifications were only in the sciences right through high school up until my college years.

3

After college I lacked the interest in working for people, and I couldn't stay at any job for more than five to seven months, I would either learn everything quickly in most cases or I would just quit. But I had an interest in creating ideas for people's business, so after a few months I gave up pursuing a bachelor's degree at another college, and just went back to work for money.

Don't ignore your calling, even when nothing else seems clear to you.

In college I was mostly known for a few things, and one was *designing clothes, and putting on concerts and doing dance performances at pageant shows.* People did not care what my academia skills were at that time. So, my question is, what are you known for today? And what do you want people to associate your name with? Always ask yourself these questions.

"If you are not willing to risk the unusual, you will have settled for the ordinary"
— ***Jim Rohn*** *(Author, entrepreneur)*

Over the years I still tried all these online trainings that are constantly being advertised, I attended all the well-known seminars, spent thousands of dollars for all these get rich programs. And they tell how you can make all this fortune using their systems, listen I am not bashing all of them, because they have to get rich somehow, right. You can listen all these gurus who know everything about anything. But that did not work for me. It can work for some people, and it might not, THE NUMBER ONE THING YOU NEED TO KEEP IN MIND TO GET TO THEIR LEVEL OF SUCCESS, IS THAT IT TAKES MONEY! Whether it's small or great, that lifestyle will require money. You might have also heard them say use "other people's money," (OPM) well that's right. Nothing is free.

Now I can tell you what did work for me, it's the information I got, and how to get where they are today and even further, and that my wonderful friends, is why I wrote this book. To share my *victories*, my **failures** and my *success* and it did not take a rocket scientist to do what I did, so I know anyone can do it.

I have interviewed many people over my lifetime, and I have always been curious to learn what is behind their why? Why do they want to work for this company? Why are they asking for a pay raise so quickly? And why are they seeking my help? Because you have to understand the reasons "why" behind anything you are building, giving, or aiding, no matter what anyone says. And the point of all this is, sometimes the reasons can either be selfish or sometimes selfless. Everything you desire to achieve or earn in life, will come at a particular time or in a particular season, so don't rush everything, learn it and then you can master it. I realize that good students usually become good employees, but self-learners normally become great employers.

> *"You can always be ready for something new, but are you prepared for it...?"*
> — ***Ralton Thompson***

Chapter 2

Identifying your Gifts and Talents

"Everything you need is already inside of you"
— Ralton Thompson

Everyone was born with a *God* given talent or gift, but most people do not use it, sometimes we cannot even identify these gifts or talents, much more to use them. In James 1:17 of KJV bible, it says *"Every good gift and every perfect gift is from above, and cometh down from the Father of lights, with whom is no variableness, neither shadow of turning."* I knew my gifts were special because of the impact I had on people. Every good thing in our lives comes from a source.

God does not change or deviate when a crisis occurs. He is still the source of all great things in our lives; so, when problems arise, remember our gifts are there to circumvent trials and find solutions. These talents and gifts were given to us for a reason, for moments like these. Yes, so you could be experiencing the worst possible situation right now or even living the best life, use every opportunity to own, to develop and even license your gifts or talents, because that is what I did. I legitimize my gifts as a business. Now I'm legal to operate professionally and spiritually.

For many generations people have died never becoming successful with their gifts or talents, and whether you want to admit it or not, many successful entrepreneurs you see today had to use their gifts or talents to amass a certain of wealth in one way another. But ask yourself, what are you doing with yours?

Everything around us is always changing and we must change with the times whether we want to or not. There are more platforms available today for people to create and expand themselves than before. Even if you're still an employee of a small or major company, a big executive in the corporate world, or even an entrepreneur to an investor, your talents or your gifts will always take you places most people will never go.

The truth is you have a path and a specific purpose for being here. In the same breath you have an adventure to embark upon, maybe something you are seeking, so having these innate strengths and unique abilities that you own will be more resourceful than anything else. While you are traveling through life, you may find yourself drawn to certain activities or things you feel you were "called to do". I have always felt this way, which is why some of us begin early to succumb to our abilities or the calling, and in that rest the keys to identifying your gifts.

I believe everyone carry within them unique qualities and attributes that provides society with nourishment. Yet, many struggle to recognize the special qualities and talents they carry, because society will NOT deem it as real importance. It may not always be obvious to you the things you have a natural aptitude for, but it can be the very same thing that you are meant to do in your life, and not what others think.

(At the earliest time possible, remind yourself and teach your children, your partner(s), spouse, or other family members that it may not appear clear now, but at your lowest level of qualification or even your highest, your experience and efforts is all relevant in this world and without you a lot of things would not be possible).

So yes, you do matter. Your life matters. And everything you do has an impact.

4 Ways to Discover Your Unique Gifts and Talents

When giving advice to others to discover anything about themselves, sometimes one answer does not suit everybody, because we're all different and many things come from self-discovery, and not others finding it for you. So a guide is always beneficent and helpful to build your self-worth and find your unique gifts.

1. Write down or make a list in your head what you are passionate about today? What drives you and get you motivated? What kind of productive things do you enjoy doing that consumes a lot of your time?

2. Always ask what is important about life to you? How and what impact do you want to have on different areas (maybe in your career, your family, relationships, even in your personal development, spirituality/religion, and innovation), make that list of all the things that are important to you in each of group.

This will give you a list of your values in regard to how you hold them. All together they will represent your life worth, so knowing your values will help guide you towards your passion and purpose.

3. Take a Self-Finder Assessment. This is a self-based interview and a procedure that will help your instinctive reactions and help you "understand yourself." This is for taking inventory of your likes, dislikes, values, personal characteristics and needs. Once you know what your primary strengths are, you can begin to leverage them for your own development and for making a positive impact in the world.

4. Start to practice and live out these traits, talents, and gifts that you have discovered. If you do not put them to the test, you will not know how great you can become or who you should be.

We are all changing constantly and sometimes it is not for the better, so we must develop the right attitude and grow into the leader, the innovator, or the pioneer that you should be.

Apply Your Special Gifts and Talents

When you have identified your gifts and talents, your passion will sometimes begin right away, so start exploring ways of how to build your life around them as well. When I started doing this, I had discovered how impactful my gifts were to others. For every day that you are alive you can become great and creative with how you can use those talents or gifts to serve yourself and others. But what does that actually mean? I believe our purpose is bigger than our simple lives.

But how can you tap into that energy of greatness and use it to make a positive impact on both the world and humanity? That answer lies within you, and for you to take that journey and find out will be amazing. But don't rush into things you're not sure about yet, take some time to contemplate on your findings and the ideas that ensued from your self-reflection and inquiry. Even from others, ask about your strengths and weakness. Plus, what are the traits that stand out for you the most as your gift or talent?

At the end of the day, whoever you are, whatever you do, and how you show up in the world, is sacred and exclusive to you. So, from everything you share whether it is a graceful presence, the advice you give, your high intellect, or your exquisite smile, they all have a ripple effect on everybody around you and elsewhere.

We do not realize how significant we are in more ways than usual. The world needs you, whoever you are and whatever you do. When you start thinking big, showing up all the time and sharing your distinctiveness, you become a role model for all of us out there.

What has happened to us as a nation and in many parts of the world, we are taught NOT to value what was given to us naturally; we only value what we were told. And we are told "we can't, or we cannot do." So many of us build another person's brand and dream; but we are not building our own in turn.

It's not bad to work a 9-5 and be contented with your paycheck, but that choice will be for the people who love their comfort zone and for others who do not want to lead a different life. There are only a few people in this world that will ever know their full worth and their value, and they are the same ones who will want to build a brand or an empire to continue to other generations.

You will be passionate about a lot of things but chose the one you are more actively involved with, because it will choose you in some way or the other. For example, you might be passionate about playing the guitar, but you're more gifted in writing music or songs, perhaps songwriting would be the preferable route, while using the guitar as a backup, everything you do will eventually go together. You always want to show your ability to commit yourself to something you believe in, and this how you follow through with your passion and using gifts or talents.

What gifts or talents do you want to brand? For you, your family and for the rest of the world to benefit from: list these out, write them down and believe me, when you have seen the impact, you can make now and, in the future, your potential to grow and to get rich is possible without any limits, *you will only have regulations, not limitations.*

*"Every great dream begins with a dreamer. Always remember, you have within you the strength, the patience, and the passion to reach for the stars to change the world." — **Harriet Tubman** (American abolitionist)*

I know it can be overwhelming how things in the world can come crashing down anytime, always changing and being unpredictable. But it is important to identify the markets to go in and how to operate with these gifts and talents in the world of business and entertainment. So, to protect you and your family, know that a job will not be an asset or security, saving up for retirement is not enough, and depending on local or federal assistance is only temporary. Even if you have a lot of money in the bank it still won't save you from *inflation* or any *crisis*.

The internet can crash anytime and so can social media and everything else behind it. But you know what will save you in a financial crisis, a pandemic or even a recession? The investment you made in yourself along with the covering of the *Most High*. Only a solid business is another safety net you can setup to garner security. But learn this, "your mind is your business, so invest in it and not minding other people's business."

There are a few professions or career path I will mention in this book that can be an asset to you, even if all of them are not listed. One is being a CPA (Certified Public Accountant) with a popular or growing business; in any crisis you would be needed. If you are a writer, artiste or performer of any caliber, your work will be a means of entertainment and education for the people. Consultants play a big part in any event; it is their service that helps to regrow and rebuild businesses. Mechanics or engineers who possess advance training and branded skills would be needed for repairs and maintenance, plus any changes needed to implement cost effective and energy conserving methods. Even if you are an investor or an entrepreneur, your business and investments will be directed in areas that you least expected them to grow and still thrive. Just remember *you are responsible for you own future, and not anyone*.

There are so many high-income resources and ways to still survive in the real world. But you have to decide what sacrifices and self-development changes must take place to get there right now. And your gifts, skills or talents can be marketed anywhere too, but remember it is your *branding* which is the reason most will say yes to you, and not just your *potential.*

What some rich people won't tell you on this journey is that you won't get rich off a salary alone, because inflation again continues to rise more rapidly along with many unexpected events. These are the same setbacks that will continue to steal your savings if you don't invest wisely. So, all the money schemes you see being advertised daily will never outlast your personal success or your means to survive in any economic downturn.

The shortest ways to success, is usually filled with unstable foundations
— ***Dr. Myles Munroe*** *(Author, minister)*

Chapter 3

Changing your Habits

"Everyone thinks of changing the world, but no one thinks of changing himself."
— **Leo Tolstoy** *(Russian writer)*

Everyone you see today is living a life they know or doing the things they want, and it's a result of their habits and their choices. I know changing our habits can seem daunting to accomplish at first, but your success will be a result of your habits too. When you think about it, we're all living out our habits each day, from the time we get up, to the way we dress, and the daily practices we indulge in. How we "think" is also habitual because we all respond to things in the world differently. If you look at it from another angle, your hobbies can actually be compared to your habits.

Habits are necessary because they got you where you are today...

We are going to focus on the "right" habits that can make you productive, healthy, and successful. But it's a choice to make that conscious decision today to free up your mind, so you can advance your life in another direction. Unfortunately for many of us, our habits can also keep us locked in a self-destructive pattern which limit our success. I am going to be honest; my transformation did not happen overnight or in a few weeks. But it took months after which it became easier, so I had to be "consistent" and dedicated without reverting to my old ways.

I knew personally becoming successful and attracting wealth was a result of changing habits. But we must first eliminate all the "bad" habits and develop new ones that are in alignment with the life we want to live.

"Your beliefs become your thoughts, Your thoughts become your words,
Your words become your actions, Your actions become your habits,
Your habits become your values, Your values become your destiny."
— **Mahatma Gandhi** *(Indian lawyer, political ethicist)*

I fought a lot of habitual battles every day that were bad, and many of us see these changes that needs to be made and won't make them. You keep saying one day, because it is easier to stay the way you are, trust me I know. The life you want to live will not materialize one day; your habits do determine your outcomes! So, start today, not some day!

What is keeping you from achieving your goals?

What are the habits you do every day that is keeping you from achieving your goals? I encourage you to be honest with yourself because these common bad habits need to be addressed.

Time management, which is very **IMPORTANT!** I used to be late for just about anything, but when you think about it, how important is that appointment to you? I began to think outside of what everybody else did, so I needed to pre-plan or schedule everything in advance, even if doesn't go accordingly, managing my time and being on time is a great habit.

Do you forget to return phone calls or text messages within 24 hours or longer? Well, I try to prioritize each call or text, to what is personal and what is business, and based on the urgency. My philosophy is each conversation is always as important as the person who made the time to call or check on you.

Staying up late without productivity and not getting enough sleep? There are so many reasons for this, but we must identify what is causing lack of sleep? Researchers, doctors and scientist will say many things, but how do you deal with lack of sleep?

14

I personally started by asking myself these questions, **is my environment safe and comfortable? Are my relationships toxic or burdensome? Am I eating right and staying healthy? Is my family doing well? Am I comfortable at my job or partying too late and not resting? And am I living a righteous life in *God's* eyes?** You name it, I use to do things no one would ever imagine me doing.

When I fixed all of these, I began to sleep better, my daily life improved and I understood my sleep patterns, and I will say this, WE ALL NEED TO SPEND MORE TIME WITH OUR SELVES and ALONE! This will help you to #SELF-HEAL, #SELF RESTORE, #SELF- MEDICATE #SELF-DISCOVER, #SELF-IMPROVE and I love this one #SERVE-*GOD*.

Do you have a habit of saying yes? When you really mean NO?

No need to show hands. You all know yourselves.

A lot of people wake up every day and convince themselves: *"this is fine, it's not that bad."* And their lives have become full of duties, obligations, debts, and schedules that demand their attention from other people, though 99% of these things are a part of our lives, it is not what we are supposed to be constantly doing.

We all cannot be people-pleaser. I remember how I felt when I said no to anyone, and I would feel bad like I was letting them down and making their lives worse. So, I kept saying yes to pretty much everything and I never had any time for myself, because I was too busy serving others. Now we must recognize what opportunities we must say yes to and the ones we say no to, because this is critical to our progress and our peace of mind.

Most days, I would get up miserable and remorseful, because I had those feelings that I was giving, and giving, giving too much. And I learned that if you continue to become that person who keeps saying "yes" a lot, you'll attract a great number of liars, cheaters, and manipulators looking to use you for their personal gains. And you'll start noticing how exhausting and joyless your life will become.

Lying and stealing are very common habits which are more difficult to stop, whether we are stealing company time, lying about family emergencies, stealing from department stores, taking our parents money, lying about what we can do, and the list goes on. These habits are inappropriate and misleading. And while some of these behaviors can indicate a deeper psychological problem for many, most of the time it is simply a common behavior that can be outgrown, but it must be unpracticed and kept under "self-control."

Proverbs 12:19 in the ESV Bible says, *"Truthful lips endure forever, but a lying tongue is but for a moment."*

So, if you lie today you have to tell another lie to cover up the first lie, then trying to remember the lie is another issue. When you take things without asking, even if you do have a guilty conscience, returning anything is also another issue.

You must become a person of *standard and principle,* less these habits won't get you anywhere credible in life. Your organization, your image, your business, and your relationships are all reflections of you and how you act.

"To see what is right and not do It, is a lack of courage." — **Confucius**
(Chinese philosopher)

Next, **learning to be committed whether it is small or great**. Do you often break promises to your friends, family members or anything of importance? I started understanding this by means of the Holy bible, in *Numbers 30:2* and *Proverb 16:3 KJV*. To explain this, if you make a commitment to do something or be supportive, it is noble and wise to stand by it, your accountability will be admired and your rewards will be matchless, so keep your word, even when you cannot always be present.

Do you procrastinate or resist planning out your day? Like most negative behaviors, procrastination is a means protecting ourselves from disappointment, and responsibilities. Mostly it involves ignoring an unpleasant task over one that is more enjoyable or easier. It's probably not the best solution but it is normal and sometimes understandable.

Procrastination is often confused with laziness, but they are very different. I had to adjust my mood and my feeling to accomplish my entire workday, having the **right attitude** is key instead of waiting for the "right moment" to act. Clean up your head space, lessen your distractions (like social media) and organize your task list, it is vital you allow yourself to focus on what needs to be done, even if it's not done in order. Apply the process!

Look at those urgent or more important tasks, maybe the follow up the appointments that you missed. Even if there are only three of them, they can still seem overwhelming; give yourself time to do each one, just knowing that you will complete them is a great start. You must design your life with the intention of feeling good and feeling productive each day, then follow your schedule and do it. You owe it to yourself, and with this you will see results and you will thank me later.

*"We spend money that we do not have, on things we do not need, to impress people who do not care." — **Will Smith** (Actor, film producer).*

Are you spending money you don't have? I get calls all the time and setup consultations with people wanting to get their finances under control, so they can stop the wasteful spending. I know firsthand it is not fun living paycheck to paycheck, not to mention how stressful it can be if you have kids! And if you're a single parent, it's a tough situation to be in. The question you need to ask is, how do I stop spending unnecessarily? Because it is a destructive habit.

I had to do what was very difficult for me, like making a weekly budget of my expenses and then setting a spending limit. Believe me this was very hard, because everything is at your fingertips, yes Amazon, eBay, and other websites. A budget sounds basic, but it was powerful. Avoid **spending triggers**, anything that will get your attention that as no value after you buy it, write it down in your brain, say it. Another tip, make the lists of everything you need in advance, not a list of "wants" and stick to it, being committed is also key, it is the foundation of staying loyal to the process. So, trust it.

Habitual addictions

How do you know if you have developed an unhealthy "habit" or if you are actually suffering from an "addiction?" It is determining the difference between the two that can be difficult, because both grow from a repeated behavior. One notable difference between habits and addictions is the *amount of time and effort it requires to change the behavior*. I believe altering your habits requires a shorter amount of time and attention, while addictions require more of everything.

Observing these patterns, I have learnt that gambling isn't real investing, alcohol doesn't give you real courage, video games isn't real life action, watching porn isn't real sex, caffeine isn't real adrenaline and social media isn't truly sociable.

The sooner we realize what is real and what is fake, the faster our advancement comes.

Imagine the Result of You Changing Your Habits

- What would your life be like if you ate healthy meals, exercised, and got enough sleep?

- What if you saved your money to invest and stopped using your credit cards unnecessarily?

- What if you stopped procrastinating, overcame your fears, and began networking with people?

- What if you created a detailed plan for success, break it down into months, weeks, and daily plans to ensure you stayed on track to achieving your goals?

- What if you taught yourself how to concentrate more to reduce stress and promote mental transparency?

Jim Kwik one of my favorite brain trainer and author, said "What you practice in private you're rewarded for in public." Wouldn't your life be different if you changed your habits and develop better ones? I bet it would! But we have to practice them until we perfect them.

Suggested steps to changing habits

My plan of action for you is to write down some productive habits you could visualize, then adopt it in your life. I say give yourself a time frame, I normally use a **21 DAY GROWTH CHALLENGE**. Start your challenge and 'act' as if you were living these new habits right now, so you could get moving towards creating more successful habits. I would like to recommend that you start four new successful habits each month, one for each week and practice them.

— Read 2 educational books or e-courses each month.

— Start eating healthy for at least 21 days (no junk food) each month.

— Start exercising 4 days each week for 21 days

— Practice to be grateful every day and not complain for 21 days, no matter how bad or challenging the circumstances are, trust the process.

Once you determine the new habits, you're ready to adopt and change, next you'll want to create a method or the methods that will support these new habits.

Here are some ideas:

1. You can make it a part of your daily visualization, like I do, by watching motivational videos and listen speeches each morning of what you want to do or enjoy.

2. You could write it on memory cards or in a notebook that you keep with you and read it several times a day.

3. You could also commit to a reliable partner or friend who has matured and reflected great habits or work with a personal coach who can help you stay on track.

4. Setup daily reminders on your phone or on your tablet to be constant and refresh it constantly, so you stay committed when you forget.

You must create and find inspiration every day to develop your new habits, less you will not grow mentally or spiritually.

All these feelings will still linger from: negative thinking, to self-criticism, self-labeling, low self-confidence to high frustration. Feeling hopeless and helpless (not being aware of your personal power). And when you're not getting anywhere productive, you become overwhelmed and start burning yourself out trying to perfect everything, this I know this from experience.

Sometimes you start getting ahead of yourself, but the fear of failure starts to swoop in. Being criticized because of the changes you're making and become alienated by your friends and even your family members. **You will have to break customs and traditions at times,** but you never need to seek approval or look outside for confirmation and be spineless. You owe this to yourself.

Just developing four good habits a month will dramatically shift your life to be more in synced with achieving your goals. The more focused you stay, the easier your bad habits will begin to change. This will shift your perspective drastically and you'll see more clearly.

Babe Ruth a professional American baseball player, famous in the 1920s. Once said "Every strike brings me closer to the next home run."

You must make that commitment to your new habits and be certain about the steps that you're willing to take in order to get rid of the old habits and adopt new ones. Don't be indecisive or unclear about how you will change your bad habits. Spell it out for yourself so you can put yourself in situations that will motivate you to act upon your new habit.

Make the decision, and then watch a new life unfold in front of you!

I want to leave you with an assignment to complete. Write down the four habits that you want to develop over the next month, and then write down the bad habits you want to stop doing.

You will leave behind who you were, start loving who are and look forward to who you will become.

> *"Challenges make you discover things about yourself that you never really knew."*
> — **Cicely Tyson** (American actress)

Chapter 4

Finding your Mentors

"Successful people ask questions. They seek new teachers. They're always learning."
— **Robert Kiyosaki** *(Entrepreneur, author)*

Everyone needs mentors or even a coach, and it has been this way since creation. If you study the greats or anyone of influence, they all have one thing in common, they were guided by a mentor and people that influence their value and gave them purpose. I know they're some individuals who assumingly think they know everything already and they can go at this thing called life alone. Well, you are wrong!

Sometimes our mentoring started earlier on in life when our parents or a family member gave us advice over a period that proved beneficial, maybe even disastrous. But during those formative years we were taught many valuable lessons. I grew up watching my mother handle any obstacle life could throw at her ever since I can remember. I am very sure she cried herself to sleep many nights because of the stresses of life, but she still got up every morning and did an amazing job to raise us in a good Christian home. She was my first superhero, and the best counselor *God* gave me for a mother.

I had many valuable teachers in my 30 years of schooling, but the reason I became more successful over a shorter period, was that I found a mentor that would help me identify my hidden gifts and talents. And my life skyrocketed into a *sundry* of earnings that boosted my value and my purpose.

I know some people cannot fathom the idea of a younger person mentoring them into success, but I have also learned that no one is above counsel or guidance in this life. Because you will not know everything and you do not need to know everything, you just need to know what will work for you. And everyone is unique in every shape and culture, because sometimes all that person is missing is that one piece, and it's a mentor.

In a world today where you can learn anything online, my best teachings still came from the lessons of a mentor and his experiences. I know all of us have imagined what our lives could be if we had all the money in the world right? But not everyone considers the "demand" that comes with it.

A successful mentor who is truthful and real with his mentees will keep it a 100% so they can be clear of the risk and dangers they are entering. Mainly of what lies ahead, but only if you chose to improve it.

"Let a man see what he can get but make him imagine what he can have."
— **Steve Harvey** *(Television host, comedian)*

I know that anyone wanting to be successful should spend more time in preparing and learning about themselves, because this will always give you leverage in the real world. Sharpening your mind and your skills is the best asset you can have before taking on a new task or any opportunity when it comes.

How can I find a good mentor?

When I decided to find my mentor, I started looking for someone who had a track record, I was not particularly looking at how much *money* they were going to help me make, but what kind of systems or training were in place for my self-productivity.

The purpose of this is to spot quality when making training decisions, not only for yourself, but for your business, your employees, and for your children. Although good mentors are usually hard to find and their training is highly desirable, not everyone has the funding or the opportunity to participate in their mentorship programs. This chapter will help clarify the roles and main responsibilities that can lead to a successful change and personal attainment from a mentor.

What to look for in a mentor?

Because mentoring is listed as the most critical factor in the career success of any mentee, mentors have many required roles and responsibilities to play, from teachers to role models, agents, counselors, and life-long tutors.

Ensure that you are in an environment where you can get an extraordinary experience and an exceptional training from your mentor. This can vary by choice too, because my recommendations are highly based on my personal preference and what I have experienced. Another thing is to have a *reflective practice* that takes you into preparing for what's ahead and stay dedicated to the training no matter what.

In addition, I would suggest that you exercise all the roles and practices given or setup by the mentor, this will stimulate your actions for better results when you practice them to perfection. Some of the roles and responsibilities of a mentor are usually identifiable in their composition of written work and experiences. Many have made a distinction between their formal training and informal training, where some explain their plans and propose ideas of what they wanted to venture in, and some were only experiments.

But some mentors had targeted goals and structured training where they had to undergo a level of change and focus to arrive at their results, all of which led to a disorderly teaching and schooling at some point. So, whether you are learning from this mentor in a systematic order or an unorthodox manner, both can make your personal development possible if you try it. But if you find a mentor who does traditional mentoring, that is great, most of them have been proven to foster a more organized development and from this their experience can build others through a set of stages.

Mentors are Teachers and Role Models

- Help the mentees improve their learning skills daily and weekly.
- Will teach the mentees the principles and knowledge of how to be the next leader in their selected fields.
- Demonstrate how to manage time and how to train and supervise any workforce.
- Provide personal development and opportunities through reading books, carrying out unusual task while using different brain hacks.
- They must show mentees how to assess information critically without being bias and do emendations on the things of high importance.
- Mentors can show the mentees how to plan properly and do research with productivity and discuss unfamiliar articles so they can exchange ideas.
- They should boost the mentees to think strategic and constantly motivate them.
- Schedule meetings for advising and giving mentees direction for their work and future careers.
- Ensuring there is timely feedback on the mentees work or the assignment.

Mentors should be agents of change and growth

All mentors should be supporting their mentees in moving forward and exploring the unknown; I believe good mentors would provide recommendations and give initiatives to set a good example of being a model citizen, both in the entrepreneurial field or in a career driven community.

Mentors must display a good conduct in training; stowing away any bad habit or bad behavior, here they should exemplify themselves in their craft.

- Good mentors will remove obstacles whenever possible without hesitation.
- They boost the mentees self-confidence and provide constant support.
- They allow mentees to try new endeavors without holding them back.
- Mentors will offer advice on how to balance a mentees professional and personal life.
- Assist mentees with the opportunity forage by recommending them to colleagues and close associates.
- Encourages the mentees to ask questions.
- Know when it is time for the mentees to advance.
- True mentors don't show favoritism, this will only create friction between other mentees.
- And mentors set the expectations for the mentees.

Mentors are Counselors

- Share experiences when they are relevant to guide the mentees.
- Listens and gives advice when asked or when it is necessary for a good cause.

- A mentor can be like a parent; and he or she will know the present maturity of the mentees and provide them with the right level of sustenance.
- Mentors protect the mentees from committing major professional mistakes.
- They must show mentees how certain situations can affect their best interests and how they should address them.
- A mentor's protection should come first in a form of preventing potential pitfalls. So, the students can prioritize their time, their commitment and not to be overburdened with the wrong activities.

Mentors are Influencers

Mentors should provide opportunities for mentees to shadow them in the field or in the line of work, at their meetings, or at conferences.

During my training I used to be right there with one of my mentors; and he would introduce me to everyone he knew. This allowed me to meet his business partners and his associates, and they were very insightful and intriguing people to talk with. It is a good discovery when you get access to their world, for it gives firsthand experience on how to secure new opportunities and other networks, which will nurture and develop your future as a mentee. When a mentor realizes that introducing their mentees to their professional world, it then increases their vision to that environment and helps them to become more self-conscious and aware.

I was fortunate to be a part of a real estate mentorship training that cost me thousands of dollars, but as a mentee in that program, I was tasked to do some research, which allowed me to avoid certain deep pits and downfall when advancing and closing desirable deals.

My mentor was genuinely interested in my entrepreneurial growth and personal development, from that he ensured that I took the right opportunities with the right people that would help cultivate and strengthen my ambitions in return.

Mentors are also seen as mentees themselves.

A lot of mentors do become life-long tutors eventually, but like many professions it is not always planned, but sometimes it happens.

- Most mentors don't let go of their own mentees; they usually stay in touch.
- Learning from their mentees brightens their outlook on life and other experiences as time passes.
- They remain supportive by attending formal events that are sponsored by them or organizations whenever possible, so the mentees can enhance their mentoring strategies and other precepts that were taught.

Benefiting from Good Mentoring?

Each role described through this chapter, is just one of the larger components in a process that promotes career development. Overall, the process is based on an apprenticeship model, in which the students or trainees works closely with the teacher to learn the science and art of his or her chosen career. The goal is for the mentees to eventually become an independent practitioner, a future leader or mentor in his or her profession.

In practice, mentors carry out their functions daily through formal and casual workings. So, seminars, workshops, scheduled meetings, and other educative forums are typical for them, all through which this development takes place.

All mentors if they believe in what they preach, and practice will invest widely in each mentee. For example, some mentors give hands-on activities from teaching how to write great business plans, task mentees with writing publications or even journal reviews, but under their tutelage and supervision. Great mentors love to show team effort approach, instead of going at it alone; there will be many instances you will have to go at it alone, but not all the time. Pay attention to everything you see a mentor does, because those are the integral parts of mentoring.

Everyone must identify the qualities they seek and any flexibility in their mentor's match, this will help you in the selection process as a key ingredient for your development and for any successful relationship. This flexibility allows the mentors and their mentees to begin working together sooner than later and still permit the freedom to find another mentor match. Because in some cases a lot of people will discover that both them and the mentor can have contradictory views or personalities, and this will lead to unavoidable chaos.

Good mentoring relationships can be more successful when the mentees and mentors create a dynamic support system. This is where the mentee feels aided but is required to have a high level of performance being exuded for the relationship to continue. This process must include an obligation to be established and it must be communicated very clearly for all the realistic expectations to be met. Mentors can run a full spectrum from observing and offering general suggestions. But the quantity and quality of any effort will still vary, depending on the mentee's drive and focus because only this will make it work effectively.

In conclusion I believe effective mentoring should be both supportive and challenging at the same time. I have seen great mentors convey their support by respecting and trusting their mentees, especially when they face many difficulties and remain optimistic because of their preparation process. This is particularly important early in the mentees career growth because the prospects of becoming truly successful are uncertain for most people. A mentor who is neither supportive nor challenging can create a roadblock to your growth, and the mentee can likely enter in an "educational disorder." And then there are the mentors who are only supportive but not challenging and will just confirm the state of the mentees mind, rather than inspiring their advancement. Just as it is with the mentors who are only challenging but not supportive, allowing the mentees to become withdrawn over time. Real growth and vision will only occur if a true mentor has the combination of both.

Chapter 5

Overcoming Fear to Build Personal Success

Fear can be real or imagined. But any kind of fear manifested always has a spiritual center.

I started to understand this through personal experiences, usually two voices will cause your thoughts, sometimes it can yours and someone else, or it can be *God* or the devil's, it's all perspective. Learn to understand your fear; I don't know what your fears are today, you could be going through a depression, having a terrible work life, regrets from a broken marriage or relationship, constantly not having peace or joy. All these will cause fear and never allowing you to become greater than the average, an average is boring. You must find the source of your fears and deal with it! That's what I did, I overcame my fears through finding the word of *God*, He became my source and inspired my thoughts, and this changed my whole life forever. So, what will change your fears and your doubts into courage?

"You must trust the small voice inside you which tells you exactly what to say, what to decide." — ***Ingrid Bergman*** *(Swedish actress)*

Before my mental change, I was physically drained from working extremely hard and not even getting close to my "milk and honey" (which was *God,* family, and wealth). I realized internally I wasn't happy; and then to make it worse I got into a "damn" car accident in October of 2018. It was so bad that the doctors ended up removing two cervical discs in my neck, I did a few minor surgeries in my lower back, and this only gave me a fraction of normalcy even to this day.

I can remember laying there in the hospital praying to *God* asking him to provide a way for me to survive this, because I had no savings and no backup plan. The realization that hit me was that nobody would remember me for doing anything impactful, and my two boys Javier and DiMari would not even have a legacy or an empire to run.

After many therapy sessions, endless doctor visits, and feeling depressed of ever working again, I picked up a book that change my entire life, yes, a book, it was the HOLY BIBLE. I knew if I wanted change, I had to become more centered, devoted and focus. What came after was mind changing; and I spent days and weeks learning about myself through this book and about the works of the prophets. The bible venerated two things for me, my *value* and my *purpose* here.

I know a lot of people might not believe in the Holy Bible, and I can understand the religious segregation in the world, but I will guarantee that one thing is true, the HOLY BIBLE is the oldest "practical and spiritual" book that was ever written. And no soul alive can invalidate that fact!

When I started reading everything that interested me, I was very fortunate to have met a great teacher by the name of Dr. Myles Monroe, who is sadly no longer with us today. Thankfully his presence was still on the internet. So, I revisited his teachings and his lectures, and I realized he had so much impact on my path that I wanted to take on his legacy.

Over the months I underwent a whole mental transformation (repentance) that opened my mind to limitless possibilities. I wanted to share this new me with everyone, but my transition wasn't complete yet, so I kept replaying this Denzel Washington quote in my head when he said, "just because you don't share on social media doesn't mean you're not up to big things, live it and stay low key, privacy is everything."

This led me to start my first consulting business in the areas where I knew I was gifted in, which boosted my earnings 7X times the amount I use to make. All from identifying what worked for me. I became a *consultant, a realtor, and an author* all in one year. Just imagine the level of hard work and dedication I had to put in, from reading to studying while being partially disabled and in pain at the same time. And not once did I ever complain that I CANNOT DO IT!

You will have many roadblocks and challenges that will arise in your life, even from circumstances with families, but it doesn't mean you don't have the P.O.W.E.R (Potential of Winning Every Race) to overcome them, sometimes losing means winning in some cases. But will this be you? From this I became a personal coach to others. I didn't plan it, but many people heard about my story and what I had went through. The advice I would give to anyone is, DO NOT INSPIRE TO MAKE A LIVING, INSPIRE TO MAKE A DIFFRENECE. Your strength will always be challenged, but your weakness will also be tested.

Leslie Brown, *American motivational speaker, and author said "you have a powerful story. It's time for the world to know about it."*

I am presenting you with two choices; you can learn how to survive through the trials and tribulations that brings success? Or you can complain and stay in your comfort zone that never thrives? Think on this, *you can be motivated to do well, but you must do well to stay motivated.* No one will hand you anything free that will last for a lifetime, everything sustainable and lasting as to be built and proven to work.

Nothing about me is self-made, I owe everything to God.

Although I was this bold and daring young man, I still had fears of venturing out into the world, fear kept me from going towards a lot of opportunities much sooner.

But I also knew it would give me a lot of experience to see what would work for me and what would not work. During my younger years in Jamaica, I was given a position as a **Quality Export Manager** for the largest private coffee company on the island, and this was a big deal for me. Because I was running all the quality checks on the products being exported to China, Russia, Great Britain and the U.S you name it, but this job was not for me, the exposure was good, and I learnt a lot, but I came under so much pressure because EVERYONE WANTED THE POSITION.

So out a *fear* of failing I stepped down and left the company. I was really good at anything I put my mind to, and this showed in my work ethic even after I moved on from many of these companies. Sometimes stepping into a new position or a role doesn't always work out how you intended it, but it was there to build and shape you. Fear only comes because it's new and unusual to you, but it doesn't last, and not all opportunities will be for you either.

Not everything out there will be taught through words or stories; you must first try to grasp what must be done to achieve all this. One day your pain and struggles will become the greatest source for your strength. So, think on where you're willing to go? Who are you willing to meet? And what fears do I need to overcome to be the first and not the next?

I never wanted to be the next Tony Robbins, the next Dave Ramsey, or the next Jeff Bezos, I only wanted to be first in anything that I felt I could excel in, and not be a shadow of another person.

Jeff Bezos the founder of Amazon said, *"One of the huge mistakes people make is that they try to force an interest on themselves. You don't choose your passions. Your passions choose you."*

When I was in college, I remember I had an Environmental Science essay to submit for this additional class grade, but the snag with this assignment was that we had to get it publish in the newspaper, so I am like what, publish where? The school doesn't even have a magazine to do that, I was already pissed and upset that I had to go out my way for this. But this was a learning lesson.

I knew I had great skills in articulating myself on paper, but I still had doubts because I didn't know what to write then and where would even publish some college kid essay? So, after a few weeks of fretting in fear I kept asking around and luckily the city of Mandeville had a small printing paper company, called the *Mandeville Weekly*, this boosted me so much to overcome my worries, so I got it publish and boom! Got my grades up.

If you start to visualize your success over your fears, you would have mentally overcome it by developing an athlete or a warrior mindset, this will possibly help you to accomplish anything multiple times before actually doing it. This type of mental outlining ensures that when your body moves, your mind was already programmed to follow its predestined path. So, fear is temporary and not real, we only keep ourselves in fear because we do not know, and we cannot know unless we try or go for it!

This same practice will prepare you to succeed at whatever you're trying to achieve.

Use these pointers to help overcome your fears

1. It is always important to gain a sense of degree of how big your fears are. Too often we get entrapped in our success or even the failure of a particular venture, that we lose sight of everything else that is valuable. I always ask myself, what's the worst thing that can happen If I don't do this or even if I try this? sometimes the reality or the after-feeling is bad, but you usually find that the *guilt* of not doing it, can be way worse than whatever you were afraid of.

2. Try to follow others and their methods. Seek out what steps they found to deal with their fears. Maybe do something that has never been done or create your own formula for someone else. You could research someone who has written work or findings on the subject; and see how you can adapt the process for your advantage. Also find someone you trust to share your struggles with, I remember talking about it consistently and doing something after made a difference.

3. Stay persistent. As the axiom goes "If at first you don't succeed, try and try again." But don't keep trying the same methods over and over; if it did not work in the past then it will not work now. Doing the same thing and expecting a different result isn't the way. I know we all can get discouraged, but try to examine the *why*, and seek a new method before you give up completely.

4. Focus on others as your motivation. Still do the things that will make you happy, so you can build up that momentum to take on the fear that comes each day. There are things we would never do for ourselves at times, but some of us would readily and fearlessly do it for others just to please them.

Grant Cardone, one of my favorite influencers and entrepreneur, mentioned, *"it's been said that FEAR stands for **F**alse **E**vents **A**ppearing **R**eal,"* which aptly implies that most of what we're afraid of doesn't ever come to pass.

5. Understand fear and welcome it. At first it may seem hard to believe or do, but fear exist to keep us safe in many ways. From different perspectives it is neither essentially good nor bad, but fear is a tool we can use to make better decisions, but NOT to rule people or get them to do unholy or self-righteous biddings.

Fear sometimes is designed to keep us stagnant, non-engaging and weak, but we must use it to help us act in ways that will generate the results we need and want for ourselves. So, embrace fear as a defense tool not a restriction and let it guide your actions, but not control you.

"Darkness cannot drive out darkness; only light can do that. Hate cannot drive out hate; only love can do that." — **Martin Luther King Jr.**

Chapter 6

Health and Wellness: The Importance of Maintaining a Healthy Lifestyle

Health education has become a trending topic over the years and research has shown that *bad health* conditions is what cause most people to die rather than actual murders. There are still some people who think that being healthy is just about the physical and it's not. Your whole entire framework must be in balance, including your mental and your emotional state. So, health watch should be part of your everyday routine because it will help preclude chronic diseases and other forms of long-term illnesses. Imagine always feeling good about yourself and taking care of your body? That's why working towards a healthy lifestyle will boost your self-esteem and your self-image anywhere. More studies have continued to show that exercise and healthy eating habits are what provide greater health benefits even beyond the weight control and weight loss most people strive towards.

In my personal research I don't think being healthy is stressed enough when working in this crazy world, and it's never too late to start, just by simply making time to do moderate physical activity, such as walking, jogging, cutting the lawn or home gardening can help prevent or delay age-associated conditions. So, ensure you focus on maintaining a healthy lifestyle that is right for your body.

In addition to eating healthy you must constantly be exercising to improve your memory especially for those with mild cognitive impairment, and it is not biased to any age or ethnicity. Every man, woman and child could ameliorate their cognitive (memory) functions if they chose to.

These benefits of physical activity can be visible and be determined over a period, but it still depends on how well everyone will treat their body.

There have been more findings where some scientists and doctors support traditional medical approaches to help prevent cognitive problems and other brain disorders. These include social activeness, taking adequate nutritional diets and doing habitual exercise which naturally contribute to improving your well-being even if you are young or elderly.

After understanding all this I realize that I needed to be functioning both mentally and physically after my accident and my road to recovery was not going to be easy. Thus, I did a whole 360 on my diet and all my favorite unhealthy food had to go, because the sacrifice was NECESSARY to achieve this. I started physical therapy, home exercise, bought all the nutritional organic foods I needed and forced myself until it became a natural routine. There are many individuals who are perfectly healthy with no chronic illness; no bodily injuries or physical impairments and they have a preferable advantage to work on themselves faster. But for anyone who is already on that path to change, then kudos to you, because you have my respect for taking up the challenge and bettering yourselves every day.

If you have access to community gyms, or just the gym equipment's please make use of them. If you work for company that has exercise rooms or walking tracks those are also a good start. Everyone should take advantage of these options. See if there is any gym or community programs that offer any wellness opportunities and get motivated. Make sure you start in your own free time but don't wait around. Try to do after-work exercise with a friend or with a weight loss support group, those will help you to go further.

Good diet and fitness

As a rule, people of all ages need to engage in a mixture of good dieting and cardiovascular exercise, muscle training and flexible body routine to maintain overall fitness and well-being.

I am not a doctor, but whatever age group you are in, you may need to modify your exercising conditions, why? Due to your body size, weight and physiological state, everyone reacts differently, and this is mostly geared towards women as a result of the hormonal changes that occurs naturally throughout their exercising sessions. I do a lot of aerobic routine such as walking, hiking, and biking. But unfortunately, I cannot swim to save my life right now, but I will one day. The other activities combined with strength training, healthy dieting and stretching all help to replace the lost muscle. The body's metabolism is revved up and this helps to keep off the weight. It is recommended for women to reduce pre- and post-menopausal symptoms, but overall, for everyone who is seeking to lower blood pressure and reduce bad cholesterol as well.

Regular exercise with good dieting will reduce the risk of breast cancer, colon cancer, kidney stones, heart disease, diabetes and high blood pressure. Plus improve your sleep patterns and help fight off depression. I have seen so many people get desirable results at their jobs they love or even ones they hated, attracted romantic relationships and other business prospects by simply heightening their physical life. These benefits are only a few rewards that good exercise brings, but you can always make your own list when you start.

Many people sometimes get bored with their accustomed routine and others might have reached their max exercising options, but there are always other means available to keep you physically active.

41

If you are just beginning a new routine for future purposes, just remember that fitness means the ability to get on with life without becoming exhausted by normal daily activities ok. So, it is very important you listen to your body and avoid trying to do too much and too soon. At the same time still do your regular workouts even if they get routinely tiresome, consistency will keep you going and get you results regardless.

All age fitness lifestyle

For many of the readers who agree that exercise is one of the life's best "natural" modifications for our bodies, it is also done by some of the world's wealthiest people. Health experts don't only recommend that we exercise to reduce excess belly flab or unnecessary fat but do it to help prevent or lower a number of life-threatening conditions, for we know that heart disease, cancer, depression, dementia and diabetes are the number one killers.

Since going through my recovery process, I have improved in many areas, even my memory started to get a little better, all attributed to healthy eating and exercising. There have been recent studies which indicated that middle-aged people who are more physically active can have a reduced risk of developing dementia and Alzheimer's disease as they get older, when I heard this, I got busier exercising, no joke, even though I am not middle-aged yet. I can understand for a lot of people the fight against weight gain and other health concerns is a never-ending battle, but the best time to prevent a lot these middle-age health crises and other adverse health conditions is now. All you must do is increase your activity by adding a few extra minutes to your regular workout until you have reached that peak of physical activity each week and you will see the difference.

Everyone should boost their physical activity before reaching middle age or older, even at your current age, these activities can still be done if you carry them out cautiously. Like going out dancing or swimming, playing sports or doing workout exercises. Even playing with your children or grandchildren will increase your overall health and wellness regardless of what shape you are in. Don't get discourage and listen to people who will say otherwise, your health comes first.

Develop brain hacks

How many people do you think notice that their entire body runs off energy? A better question, how do feel when you eat certain food afterwards? The body as to be fed properly largely the brain because it will engender more satisfying results from the right kind of food it gets. As my dear friend O'Neil Clarke would say, *"brain power is the main power."* Studies have shown eating good nutritional food will nourish the brain and decrease the chance of depression significantly. In most cases a lot of people have too many options and chose not to eat healthy, for example most people don't realize that eating too much *sugar filled food* which causes more depression. I started eating healthy years ago but added more to my diet since the car accident and it has reflected changes in my body functions and how energize I feel.

Honestly, I don't like eating some of these brain foods sometimes, but it works, and if I didn't, I wouldn't be promoting it. On my list are blue berries, eggs (remove the yoke if you want to lower excess cholesterol) green leafy vegetables, salmon, avocadoes, turmeric, broccoli and dark chocolate with many other *natural organic* foods. These will give your brain nutrients and fuel the body with the energy it needs.

Jim Kwik who is a brain trainer talked about a technique we can use to provide healthy brain functions called **'killing ANTs'** which stands for **killing Automatic Negative Thoughts.** These are present everywhere and surface most times when we face challenges or just about anything. We must practice not to harbor negative thoughts that will rule our lives, I know you cannot ignore it, but you can definitely control it. When you try to eliminate all negatives thoughts every time they arise, you start to become what I call *mentally limitless*.

Another means of healthy brain function is **brain protection.** This is detrimental to all your success if you want it. Name anything and it's the brain that controls it. I used to play a lot of sports growing up from soccer (football), to cricket, college basketball and then American football shortly after I migrated to the U.S. I had so many minor injuries, I had to stop playing over the years. You may ask why? Well see I love my brain and I don't want any carelessness and unprofessional playing to damage it. So, depending on your lifestyle and your recreational activities, I would encourage anyone who loves daring, hard contact or extreme sports, not to indulge in them very often. These are high risk games for death and damage to the most "valuable asset" you have the money maker called the brain.

Getting access to fitness resources

If you are living in a remote area that lacks certain fitness amenities or maybe there is transportation concerns, don't be discouraged. Start with free fitness videos on the internet, do some easy floor exercise's which is way more cost-effective, or you can try other alternatives like hiring an expert instructor in the privacy of your home. You can still find at-home fitness resources such as workout DVDs, CDs or Blu-ray disc even if they seem outdated, especially when internet access is limited, or none is present at all.

It goes without saying: No matter how old you are, or how young you are, consulting with a health care professional is my wisest advice but beginning any type of physical fitness program is still a choice of your own. If you want to get productive and stay energetic, here are a number of suggestions for doing that and stay on point:

1. Maintain regular exercise pattern

Even if you don't force yourself into any intense workout, it is vital to keep as active as possible and I can't stress this enough throughout this chapter. Keep yourself moving by doing some household chores. Just do what your body allows you to do, simple.

What is always important is that you continue exercising. Give yourself at least twenty to thirty minutes (20-30) a day to stretch or move actively, whether the time is cold or hot, exercising for a minimum of three to five times a week is always a good sign. If you can't stick to it; try to have enough physical activity each day.

2. Be 'compos mentis' in your diet

To maintain a healthy lifestyle, you need to have consistency and discipline, and to do this you need to have full control. Start by adding more fruits and vegetables to your diet, eating fewer carbohydrates, lowering the high sodium and unhealthy fat. While specifically avoid eating too much junk food and *sweets* as possible. It sounds hard, but it is not. Avoid skipping a meal—yes! This will only make your body crave for more food the moment you start eating again. Remember it is best to burn more calories than you eat.

3. Surround yourself with positive energy

We must surround ourselves with positive energy in order to have a healthy mental and physical state, because not all problems can be avoided. This will help you to face many stumbling blocks with an optimistic viewpoint. Also keep encouraging friends and other people around you to help tweak your decision making and castigate any unhealthy lifestyle you're developing.

I have personally been exercising this method of positive thinking for several years and now I am experiencing more health benefits than before. One theory is that having a positive outlook enables us to cope better with stressful situations, which then reduces the harmful health effects of stress on our body. It is also considered that positive and optimistic people tend to live a healthier lifestyle than others who don't practice this. Ensure you follow a healthier diet by all means necessary, don't drink or smoke alcohol in excess or simply don't pollute your bodies at all.

Maintaining a healthy lifestyle sometimes can be difficult, but it does not always require a lot of work. Just keep doing what you do best to stay fit and apply the healthy tips I listed, along with what works for you, then you will be a productive individual in no time.

4. Engage in the things you are passionate about

Choose anything that will genuinely excite you and it doesn't have to be job related either, I can tell you I was never the one who felt passionate about working on holidays. But don't get me wrong, the extra pay might be great for some people, I just believe it's better to find activities that will keep stress off and allow you to take breaks easier. This way you can do something that you love as a positive relief, and it will improve your mind and your body as well.

46

When you find a passion that you're enthused about, it becomes more enjoyable for you to indulge in. Always be sure that the passion you're committing to will provide the right health benefits you're looking for. Because if it doesn't help you release any discomfort, stress, or anxiety, then it isn't right for you especially when you are around people.

Practicing Self-Care Skills

I believe it is very essential above many things that we seek to take care of our mental state then the physical daily, particularly when you are in a demanding environment. A few basic suggestions I can give to help prevent bodily deterioration, if you're an over-achiever or a workaholic.

Examine your body. A lot of us, specifically men sometimes don't check their bodies very often for signs of blisters, cuts, or calluses, etc. Some women wear tight shoes or tight clothing for beauty but end up worsening their pain and it leads to sores that won't heal quickly. Your comfort is detrimental to your function so in every way protect it.

Avoid prolonged pressure. If you are sitting or standing uncomfortably over a period, it will reduce the blood supply to the muscles and increase the pain and fatigue in the legs, back and neck. Look at the professions that encourage these practices? And take notice of the results people usually get after doing these jobs. The unbalanced practice of not being health conscious when working in certain fields will raise a number of health concerns. From obesity to high blood pressure, high blood sugar, excess body fat around the waist and abnormal cholesterol levels which make up a cluster of conditions referred to as metabolic syndrome. Even without doctors or research your body will show you these signs.

THE UNUSUAL PATH TO SUCCESS

Another tip, try to avoid keeping pressure on your knees when you crossed them or lean on your elbows for an extended time. This is a typical habit for most people although it might seem courtly or poised to do; in some instances, doing it extensively may cause nerve damage after a while.

Get massages often. This is not a common practice for everyone, but massaging your entire body regularly gives you a deep feeling of relaxation and calm. This occurs from the brain releasing chemicals called endorphins (neurotransmitters) that produces the feeling of wellbeing. Massages are so important that it decreases high levels of stress hormones, such as cortisol, adrenalin and norepinephrine that impair the immune system over time. When you realize that it helps to improve your circulation, stimulate the nerves and temporarily relieve certain pain and discomfort, you will think twice about refusing a massage next time. So have someone you trust to massage your body, or you can just schedule spa visits or hire in a professional.

Confession and resolution. Confessing to someone that you are unwell or admitting that you have some negative aspects of your life that needs changing is a start, but don't dwell on these matters alone. I have managed to move forward and become more positive after finding out what works best for me. You might be thinking there is nothing positive about you confessing, but there are lessons in everything. Be thankful if *God* has blessed you with no illness and any health concerns. Perhaps your outlook on life can increase self-awareness for others or give them support to maintain a healthier lifestyle.

Seek and accept support. If you are struggling with any issues whether it is personal or financial, it can sometimes lead to poor decisions, and I know many people believe asking for help is a sign of weakness and will reject it.

Not all of us can get the support we want from family members or friends, because different situations might warrant for different things. I still remember the pain and suffering I went through after my mother died, while recuperating from a major surgery three months before. It was a new trial that I alone had to deal with. I thought about joining a support group although some support groups are not for everyone, my next option was going to a therapist because I knew some of their techniques and treatments could help. My advice to you is to go someplace that you can meet the right people who will understand what you're going through and guide you over time.

Get out the house or the apartment. It is natural for some people to want to be alone. We have so much in our daily lives to deal with from major health issues to bad relationships, losing friends and family members, or just simply going through depression and stress. But this only makes it easier to dwell on the pain and the regrets. Instead, go out more often, visit the park, go to the beach, see a movie, or take a trip somewhere. Regaining control and developing a relief program that works for you is the way forward. Ensure you maintain your optimum fitness and well-being whether you're in your home or outside of it.

There are always so many non-human distractions that will arise and these I call "modern day health villains." The biggest one is the *internet,* and it is sometimes the hero but also the villain. We see a lot of information being manipulated and influence through the internet, causing this digital overload in our brain most times. And I mentioned earlier in *chapter 3* that we need to spend a lot of time with ourselves to have clarity and focus. But by doing this we have to detach our minds from the worldly things to find that peace and tranquility. (John 14: 27)

Many people will form and speculate a particular lifestyle or way of life for you, but it doesn't mean it will fit your goals or purpose. A less dependency on digital assistance, such as the phone, tablet or computer will allow you build up better cognitive abilities (these are brain skills to gather knowledge and retain information naturally). This separation will return us to be more proactive and effective without using excessive digital aid.

Research has also shown that people can become poor or bad decision makers when they can't think for themselves. We should know that our creativity is inside of us, not on a digital device. In the beginning I was never tech savvy or incline to use digital devices, so I have mastered not having an addiction for it. But when I do need to start a project, I would write it down on paper first and then go create the idea on the device. Another notion I will debunk for many people who believe that we can multitask, is the fact that our brain was only design to focus on one task at a time. It might seem like you are multi-tasking, but you CANNOT COMPLETE FIVE (5) TASK AT ONCE effectively. You're not a machine, but go ahead try it, then see where it gets you.

Chapter 7

Mastering the Laws of Attraction

Whatever you hold in your mind on a consistent basis is exactly what you will experience in your life. — **Tony Robbins** *(Coach, author)*

There are movies and books that may have you believing that the Laws of Attraction are something new in our time. But the truth is these laws have been around since ancient days. In fact, the Bible provides clear instructions on how to use these laws and show occurrences when they are in action.

The laws are centered in our creator and a lot of people might have mastered using them, while some are still trying to understand how the Laws of Attraction work. To explain this tentative subject in my view, I believe to master anything even the Laws of Attraction; it is more about the method in which you apply it and not mainly about the results. Because results can either be good or bad, that is why we must always be careful of what we wish for.

Most of us can work and save money to buy anything we want, even to win the lottery which is still by chance. But getting certain results doesn't necessarily mean that you are using the Laws of Attraction consciously. You might get confused thinking it's the laws you're using when it's not. The stuff we "think" on can usually be influence in a particular order, so it doesn't mean it will manifest itself into existence, like "think and grow rich" it doesn't work like that. Our dreams and ideas are far more evolved and complex than any materialistic possession, even when we choose a career path.

"All that we are is the result of what we have thought." — **Buddha** *(Founder of Buddhism)*

In my research I do believe our "visions" are the most powerful manifestation you can create in the mind. If we have a clear understanding of how we want to live our lives, then the people who we want to interact with and share those opportunities with, will come closer to these visions or they will be drawn to us as well. To maximize this powerful method, I have surmise that we need to make a habit of using our visions to reach the success we dream of and work towards it with prayer and planning.

Here are few a realistic signs and practices that show you are trying to master the Laws of Attraction, or you already have.

1. You have high expectations, even if it turns out not going in your favor.

Many of us have become more realistic of what can be achieved by not limiting our belief system, while on the other hand, some people still limit their thoughts. A masterful student can be more hopeful than the doubter, and still see the sublime possibilities of many things that the average person would not see using the law.

The Laws of Attraction usually gives what is *expected,* and not what you always *want*. Hopefully this makes sense. If it doesn't, I'll say it like this, I **want** my book to reach 70 million homes or more in the next 5 years, but in truth and in fact it might only be **expected** to reach 700,000 homes, maybe more or less. Either way I am always optimistic.

2. You generally have a positive attitude and avoid gossiping and complaining.

A masterful performer of the law will regulate what comes in and out of their lives, because we are naturally responsible for our own peace and sanity. In short, people must understand that they will have to deal with their own drama, regardless of where it comes from. And this is where you must have a FILTER CONTROL from them. Not all problems will be solved in life and most people will continue to blame their issues or unfavorable circumstances on other people. In return, you should revert to your own safe space and allow some drama to pass you. I believe to improve anyone's quality of life and even yours, it is best to keep a positive attitude. Even when it's difficult, a masterful performer tries to always stay positive.

3. You tend to get along with more people.

This might come as a surprise, but when you avoid gossip and drama, you start to notice how well you get along with people more than you would imagine. I see this as the mindset and an attitude skill. One of the more *adroit* skills set a student can master with this law, is to become sociable and *evasive* at the same time. You will even start appearing different from everyone when you do this. And think about it, how many people do you know that are like you out there? Exactly.

4. You can disconnect from the outcome and move on quickly.

The problem with getting results or dealing with disappointment sometimes, lie where too many people become emotionally attached to the situation or to the decision they made. You have to practice disassociating yourself from this, even if you lose or the decision you made did not go as planned.

Start by mastering ways of how to stress less and avoid more distractions affecting your function, it's best to let it go and focus elsewhere even if it's temporary than to be stuck in the same place.

5. You will experience high levels of synchronicity.

Carl Jung coined the term in the early 1920's but in order to understand this it's an experience that has to be lived more like experiencing serendipity. A masterful performer who does this will see their vibrational alignment when they spend a lot of time creating good energy and meaningful thoughts. This now brings about a desire in reality from synchronicity.

Now, synchronicities would be simultaneous occurrence of events, like thinking about a friend or a family member and suddenly you receive a call or a text from them. It can be going to a store and looking for a specific item but instead you find another item you have been searching for a longtime, not having any thought you would find it there. When we are aligned, we emit positive thoughts into our reality quickly and these manifestations can occur on a regular basis.

> *Imagination is everything. It is the preview of life's coming attractions.*
> — **Albert Einstein** *(Theoretical physicist)*

6. The way you observe the world is changing drastically.

For you to catch sight of this, you would have to be conscious and intentional in mastering the Laws of Attraction, this then unveils the systems that were hidden and setup to limit your abilities. Exposing your surroundings to what most millennials call today being "woke."

Anyone who understands what is possible without limitations will practice this and know that they only exist in our minds. Usually, it causes us to experience a dramatic shift in the way we view life, our relationships, our jobs, rules, the health system, governments, and everything else we are taught in society.

7. You create your own reality.

A masterful performer will start to design a different life when they experience a preeminent shift to change what's old into something new. The Laws of Attraction will make it very natural for you to restructure your home-life, your career, your relationships even your own personality. This newfound realization might come as a result of you discarding the old non-essential beliefs and systematic programming that once kept you and everyone else in an unsatisfactory environment.

These changes are oftentimes intentional, but moreover they can come unexpectedly from self-reflection or self-discovery within oneself. For example, you might become inspired to quit your job for something new, like starting a business. You could find yourself unexpectedly replaced one day or laid off from your job, although in that moment it can be discouraging and hurtful. A masterful performer will create his or her safe space to look beyond that and seek the rewards moving forward.

8. You will see the benefits in a problem or a negative situation.

While so many people can have a negative thought towards an unpleasant encounter or setback. A masterful performer does not view it with prejudice. They understand and realize that negative moments and situations can provide invaluable guidance or correction where needed.

Everyone should understand that they're in control of their own problems and never let these problems control them. After you have eliminated this belief, a masterful performer will dominate or control his or her situation. Out of this process can birth a mindset which adjusts you to become more equip than before and can deal with any outcome. Remember you cannot control or stop every problem or negative situation that arises. That's why many people get caught up in their own problems and completely miss the opportunities for growth.

*"You have power over your mind – not outside events. Realize this, and you will find strength." — **Marcus Aurelius** (Roman emperor)*

9. You understand that life is a journey, and not a destination.

Not many people will appreciate that life is a journey and not just a destination to *riches and great health*. A masterful performer will set their minds and spirit solely on matters of character and integrity. These qualities are eternal and not those of sensation and vanity which will pass away easily over time. All life experiences are journeys we go on and it's not a station; it's a road. And it's not a rest stop for the transient enjoyments like (*sex, money and power*) which are merely the little rest-stops upon the roadside of life, where you are refreshed for a moment, but never satisfied.

You must continually seek what is still before you; I call it "where faith meets purpose." A masterful creator understands this even with all the success they have attained, it was not unforeseeable in reaching that "place of Zen," but it was by design and planning. A masterful creator appreciates the journey over the destination.

Because 9 times out of 10 it doesn't really exist, it is just another step towards the next manifestation you will create.

10. **You find your place in the equation.**

When you realize you have mastered many skills that sets you apart from regular individuals, they will sometime struggle to grasp what you can do. But this is a part of the bonus in the creative process. A masterful performer sticks to the things he or she knows they can do well: so, identifying your desires and your passion will get you into a vibrational position to see this. You then allow the universe (or the "Source" *God*) to do the job by delivering the fruits or rewards of your manifestations.

There will be no need to figure out how something will come your way, because the signs will be obvious and only to you. It will be as King David said in *Psalm 23* KJV "The LORD is my shepherd; I shall not want. You will have all the requirements ready to identify and position yourselves so that the manifestations and the work you put in will bring them to you. Not falling from the sky but from the places you will go to, people you will meet and from the opportunities that will come.

If you can reach to the place of restitution mentally, then there is no need to worry much about "how" and "when" it's going to happen. Because a masterful performer will know that the things he or she desires will come in an "unusual" way from the higher source.

11. **You understand what YOU want and stayed focus on it regardless of what anyone says.**

Many people are program to think we should be rich or famous and have a great marriage in order to be viewed as successful, all these things are great, yes. However, a true performer takes a much more subtle and personalized approach in creating the life they desire, not the one carved out or designed for them.

It may seem normal to fall in que, but when you have mastered the Laws of Attraction and set your focus on the desired goals or purpose. The things you sometimes go after may seem strange or unimportant to others, because you care less right now and seem unbothered with maintaining the status quo. This will allow you to go on a personal journey of self-discovery and expansion, not to prove your powers to everyone else, but to enjoy and live the best life you can create.

12. Mastering the Power of Attitude.

A true performer demonstrates how positive attitude can boost their energy, increase their inner strength, inspire others, and build the courage to meet difficult challenges.

Here are several ways to adopt a positive mental attitude while using the Laws:

Be a positive thinker. I don't know how many people do this, but develop a *self-talk template*, what this does, it controls all the endless stream of unsaid thoughts that run through our heads every day. These automatic thoughts can be positive or negative sometimes and they come from your rational behavior and your experiences at times. Other self-talk thoughts may arise from misunderstandings we create but usually because we lack information or jump to conclusions.

Surround yourself with positive people. I have mentioned so many times throughout the book that having positive people around is a healthy and functioning part of your life. You must spend time with the people who are productive and supportive whether at your workplace and in your home so they can embolden your spirit. Be careful not to get too close to people in sinking sand, because they might pull you down faster while you are there trying to help them out. Always remain on a solid ground for only then can you be the rock on which they stand.

If it so happens that you are constantly surrounded by negative energy either from family members or friends, then you have to become that positive force for yourself, and then let them feed off of your energy, but don't let them drain it.

Practice dealing with criticism. This will be one of the more difficult mental techniques you will have to try, owing to the fact that it's attached to our emotions. Because you can't escape critical and judgmental people who will come after you, start to adopt ways in dealing with rejection and criticism daily. In doing this I suggest a method I regard as "mental assertive defense." M.A.D, yes it might seem funny, but act M.A.D when people come for you in every way that's negative and unconstructive.

To master this process, is to conduct a *self-therapy conditioning*, where you pretend to play out every negative conversation between you and yourself, maybe a friend or a close family member, just be creative. You must practice building up your assertiveness, conditioned responses, and your own defensive mechanism against possible criticism that you can face. These mental skills are then transferred to the real world through real life encounters and experiences both past and present. And from these pre-construct exercises you will see results and how they affect you afterwards.

Be kind to yourself. If I didn't learn how to appreciate my life in so many ways, I would not be able to enjoy my own company most days. It is unfortunate that a great number of people say and do the meanest things to themselves and over *exacerbate* some situations long enough until they start to believe it. Don't be so hard on yourself for anything, the world has enough negativity to drag you down already, so don't add to it.

Keep it in perspective. I believe our lives should be about highlighting the things that matters the most to us and focusing all our efforts in these areas. Like building relationships, family, being responsible and working on yourself. The trivial things that can go wrong, don't always get you down each day. So, when you find peace within yourself, become the type of person that can live at peace with others. And then learn to address or ignore small issues and move on.

Turn challenges into opportunities. First be mindful of how often you expose yourself to the negative messages from the news, social media and from peers or family members, especially if you can't handle it. Your challenges will come from the things that sometimes you don't have control over, so keep your exposure to a minimum, but stay informed with enough information. This will help you to be steps ahead of the outcome in most instances.

Always keep a mental list of the ways any current crisis or challenges are impacting you or your life. For example, "I'm concerned about losing my job", or "Sales are down and the business is slow." Instead of letting these challenges overwhelm you, turn them into opportunities. (Rather than hitting the wall, climb over it or go around it, there is always another way).

The challenge: I'm concerned about losing my job. **The opportunity:** Get your resume updated and start networking to find a rewarding and fulfilling job that you have been thinking about pursuing for the last five years.

Next challenge: Sales are down, and the business is slow. **The opportunity:** Use this slow period to get your business organized and restructured, update your marketing strategies, build new connections, and reconnect with past customers that you had no time to call, reinvent yourself and the business image.

Finally, count your blessings. One of the most humbling attitudes you can have is to be grateful for anything special in your life, rather than taking them for granted. We can simply do this by giving thanks when we wake up in the mornings, saying grace over our meals, keeping written affirmations in a journal, or posting items on social media.

Some of the greatest possessions in life aren't material things but seeing every opportunity to make a wonderful memory each day.

I am no longer cursed by poverty because I took possession of my own mind and that mind has yielded me every material thing I want, and much more than I need. But this power of mind is a universal one, available to the humblest person as it is to the greatest. — **Andrew Carnegie** *(American industrialist)*

Chapter 8

The Influence of Success

"I never dreamed about success, I worked for it." — **Estée Lauder**

Estée Lauder was an American businesswoman and cosmetics pioneer. Founder of the self-named cosmetic line and is recognized as one of the most influential self-made businesswomen in the United States.

Most people have a strong desire to be successful; however, what they don't see is what goes into the process. While many might want to be an overnight sensation, a "positive" influential success DOES NOT COME QUICKLY, nor does it come overnight. Statistically it is so rare that I believe more people might have a better chance winning a scratch off game or the betting on a football match, than to get to any level of success without working for it. The internet along with social media has only highlighted these events faster in recent years, but do not be misled that by this type of mindset, because it will not have any longevity in trying times or in a crisis.

Ask yourself, what happened to all these overnight sensations today? And are they still around? See there is a major difference in being famous and staying famous at the same time. *What most people call overnight success is just the market realizing the value of a great product or service in that moment.* And the business or the individual's gifts, skills or services was only enshrouded for a while and then it suddenly emerges on the scene.

Fun fact: Did you know that the humble beginnings of Adidas, today one of the largest sportswear companies before Nike, began manufacturing shoes after World War I in1924.

And it was not until 1936 at the Berlin Olympic Games that African American track-star Jesse Owens wore his shoes to win four gold medals that were reportedly given to him as a gift from the founder Adi Dassler. Owens's single-handedly increased the awareness of the Dassler's brand around the world in just one day from the medal-winning performance. So, would you call that overnight success? No, that is preparation meeting opportunity again.

We must know the difference between overnight success and early success. A lot of people today misread the achievements of entrepreneurs, actors, artiste, musicians, athletes, and authors for sudden accomplishment. We may find it unreasonable and even unfair, that someone else can become a millionaire at age 17, 21 or 25. But many have dedicated years to learning and perfecting their art or craft, while experiencing a lot of failures, racial injustice, and resentment before finally being successful.

Those who are celebrities today along with people of high caliber or influence, also endured their fair share of trials and errors for years; many of which was not publicized or televised. We cannot be jealous of those who had a faster route to success than some because their success is not your success, and their rewards, are not your rewards. Their wealth is only theirs unless they share it and we do not know what *sacrifices* they had to make for that ultimate life on earth.

To conclude this belief and move on, the idea of overnight success is delusional. And for those planning their life around this notion will be doomed.

Now influence is an effect and not a position or status. This also does not come from the brilliance of your ideas. Influence comes from your ability and the capacity to create a strong personal presence to change the lives of the people and the followers around you. Through my personal success story, I discovered some elements proven to help you achieve the best life you can have both personally and professionally. When you carry these out, it can set you in the right direction to accelerate your goals and your true potential.

As an Influencer you want people to know who you are and that you care about them. Even more, you want them to act on it, by learning and engaging from your content. I tell my friends and people in general that they should not be impressed by money, power, and titles, not even looks. But be impressed by integrity, humility, kindness and gratitude. Your success is dependent on what the consumers and the followers deem as good or bad, not you; no matter how much material you put out or the content create. *You have to pay attention, because attention then pays you in return.*

They must want the products and services to join in, making their lives a lot better while empowering them at the same time. Because your purpose is to build them better businesses, provide them with live-changing results, give them high energy entertainment and inspiring healthier relationship goals for a better world, it's not always about you, it is mainly about them.

Napoleon Hill, which is best known for the book, *Think and Grow Rich*, said **"The ability to influence people without irritating them is the most profitable skill you can learn."** His book is considered as the most influential self-help books of this generation. So, we have to create an influence that will impact people lives, whether we are dead or alive.

How to thrive in any season without traditional marketing methods

Has anyone seen a brand so popular they don't need to advertise? Well, if your answer is yes, then you are correct. There are a lot of companies like that out here and even people of influence who don't need the publicity to survive. To be honest, some people still think there is no such thing as a brand or a company that doesn't advertise or wouldn't want to advertise. Not knowing they are super successful will surprise the hell out of you today. Probably you're thinking how anyone can do this. Again, nothing is humanly impossible if you want it that bad, just ensure it doesn't take away the joy from the experience.

A lot of us today live for the excitement of being wooed by the big brands. But as a Consultant, I like to figure out new and innovative ways to satisfy my client's needs because I am only one person, and I want them to know I'm always there if they need me. This process takes much work and smart calculative planning, because to be set apart from every brand and anyone of influence, you simply must know "how" to hand out your marketing dollars and "who" you give it too.

Most of these companies and brands try to avoid the best marketing practices that are mainly use today, so they can generate an unusual "buzz" and this intrinsic identity which makes each one of them uniquely different. So, start by being different in all your ventures of life, from your business to your art, you will stand out more when you don't try to fit in with everybody.

Here are few brands that don't do the traditional marketing, research them, and see what you can learn from each one.

1. Zara

This company's brand and influence is well renowned today, they are a Spanish apparel retailer who was operating under the name Inditex but later renamed themselves as ZARA marking the first store setup in 1975. Since then, they have managed to open about 6,500 stores across 88 countries and solely built an empire based upon their *reputation.* As an international company they had the technology and automation which allowed them to examine the trends and consumers reaction so they could get fashion from the runway to the racks in a matter of days, this system took great timing and preparation.

Zara was able to give up traditional marketing strategies in a few ways. First, they target men, women, and children in highly populated cities. Second, they produce cheap, fashionable clothing, with a high attention to detail. And third, they only produce a limited number of each piece to create a sense of urgency among their consumers. They've also mastered the art of influencer marketing. This was done when the Duchess of Cambridge gave the brand a huge international promo when she wore one of their brand dresses a day after her wedding to Prince William.

Key takeaway for your brand or business?

Target the products or services you are great at and don't be afraid to rely on word of mouth, try to foster an influencer channel that is loyal to your brand and in time you will grow. Today, you'll find more traditional marketing channels available to Zara's fans (like Instagram, Pinterest, and Facebook, etc.) but the retailer built its empire with a well-placed retail, on-trend offerings, and some serious word-of-mouth.

2) Trader Joe's

Trader Joe's is an American grocery food chain who is headquartered in California, USA. The company became so competitive that they started to lead in the "fresh appearance" for grocery stores in the United States by 2015. Around November of 2019, Trader Joe's had already opened over 503 stores in 42 states.

The first Trader Joe's store was opened in 1967 by founder the Joe Coulombe in Pasadena, California. But it was then owned by the German entrepreneur Theo Albrecht from 1979 until his death in 2010, leaving the ownership to his heirs. Many people might not be aware but the German supermarket chain ALDI Nord, is the parent company to which Trader Joe's belongs and they also follow the same principle of not exercising the new age of marketing strategies.

However, to keep current with the millennial trends, Trader Joe's has maintained an online presence with a website and social media platforms, but you won't find them doing traditional advertising like Walmart, Whole Foods and other grocery chains. The business model that they have managed to create over time as allowed them to catch on to their consumer's interest.

There have been various articles on Trader Joe's business model stating how it is eye-catching and unique to the point where they isolate themselves from the branding illusion, to have a ubiquitous influence in the market. The company makes the customers shopping experience so inclusive and clear-cut, that there was no other comparison of grocery retailers in the U.S and in the world because of how they showcase their products. Withstanding all this, things can change in the future for Trader Joe's model, but to date they have had great success so let's see what the future holds for them.

Key takeaway for your brand or business?

Become so attractive in every aspect of your business or branding that people cannot get enough of the products and services, which should be affordable, of great quality and available at their convenience, this will propel you into more markets. Buying directly from the manufacturers or being the source will give you a better advantage over the markets. This way you control it and when pricing the products as well.

You can start with traditional marketing and pay for advertisement to get you some recognition. This will then give you more advantage of how to price the products or your services on a scale that is seriously affordable and warmly attractive. You must aim to build a brand or company that is uniquely different, oftentimes we're so afraid to give up what is expected in the marketing world, and take the road less traveled by others. If you take a chance on yourself, I believe you could create a *one-of-a-kind customer experience* for everybody.

3. Automobili Lamborghini S.p.A.

Lamborghini is an Italian manufacturer of luxury sports cars and SUVs Company based in Italy. They are currently owned by the **Volkswagen Group** through its subsidiary **Audi AG**. There are many iconic cars out there that have brought interest to different generations. A lot of stunning automobiles made it throughout history; but there's something about Lamborghinis that just stands beyond the significant historical wonder. The moment the Lamborghini name is mentioned, many of us automatically think of the vertical doors which was introduced to the world and popularized by the Lamborghini *Countach*. However, Lamborghinis have so much more than what meets the eyes.

To understand why Lamborghini is so special, you need to know a little bit about its history and the creator. It was first invented out of a "need" just like most innovations and creative work because problems require a *solution*. But the journey of the brand wasn't always smooth sailing. Before Ferruccio jumped into the world of GT cars, he was a manufacturer of tractors and other agricultural machinery.

He managed to capitalize on the overt "demand" left in the industry after the war. From this he made a fortune out of his business and rewarded himself with a new *Ferrari*, which was the standard in the sports car manufacturing arena at the time. Being the perfectionist that he was, Ferruccio was dissatisfied with the car's subpar clutches, and this birthed a new idea.

Enzo Ferrari who was the founder totally dismissed Ferruccio's claims and told the tractor maker "to go back to making tractors and leave the sports cars to the experts." It was funny, but in a situation like that most people would get discouraged and throw in the towel, right? But Ferruccio took it on as a challenge and began to work on what would be the first Lamborghini ever made. Many individuals at the time did not know that Ferruccio himself was a gifted engineer and mechanic, and most times your action should speak louder than words. For that reason, Lamborghini has been known to be the makers of the best internal combustion engines in the industry. And that statement remains true to this day, as the company continues to push pass boundaries under the ownership of the Volkswagen Group.

Lamborghini company said in a press release "we don't do commercials because our target audience isn't sitting around watching T.V." A lot of people will take that as an offensive statement, but ask yourself, what target audience do I want for my brand or my business?

Key takeaway for your brand or business?

The reason we don't see Lamborghini or most rare expensive luxury cars doing TV commercials, is for an obvious fact, because the people who can afford them don't sit all day watching T.V. and it's simple. Think about the ways you could create urgency for your customers to buy your product? And make it appealing to them, whether they watch T.V all day or not?

For starters, I would setup a membership or a *system* that could provide a built-in channel of qualified leads and prospects, then share any exclusive discounts or offers, maybe after I could expect a higher rate in return.

Note: Lamborghini doesn't advertise their business on TV, but they do have social media. Their customers only represent a mere number of the viewership. So, they would be paying an absurd amount of money to reach the 99% of viewers who may not be able to afford what they're selling now. And as I have mentioned, there are more than one efficient and economical way to target your customers or client just based upon your services.

If you want to be influential in a particular area of life, whether using your gifts or your expertise; try following my steps as your guide. And if you manage to develop a system along this path that will impact your success, then you will have great acclamation both locally and internationally. In business, you don't have to accept what the market determines as a good product, because if you can improve the standard of anything for everybody, then I encourage you to go for it.

*Pay the price today, so you can afford it tomorrow...— **Ralton Thompson***

Create a strong personal brand:

We all should know what a personal brand is; it is your signature look, style or trademark for which you are recognized. Mainly it is what people think about when they see you, like Jamaican sprinter Usain Bolt, who won 8 Olympic Gold medals. He's known as the fastest man in the world today, but he as a signature move at the end of each race, and every track star fan is familiar with this when he does the lightning bolt pose.

Having a strong personal brand is essential to influence. When people know they can count on you, and know what you stand for, they are more likely to listen to you and "support" your ideas and your products.

Barbadian singer and businesswoman Robyn Fenty, popularly known as Rihanna, has a huge following in the music and fashion industry. Though Rihanna has won multiple awards, she started a luxury fashion line that became so successful it increased her net worth to over 1 billion U.S. dollars and still climbing from all her influence.

Enhance your network:

A key part of having an effective brand or following is to have the right people know about you. And the right people are the ones that can help you build an online presence, create movement of your services and get things done in your company. It is important for you to be well connected in everything, so start by building a genuine connection with your peers, trustworthy people at your workplace, and with those in your business. Because sourcing the best interests will only cultivate and expand your contact network.

Building a network around good people to support you is a hot commodity, for some it will not come easily, but with constant effort and determination you have to keep trying. On your way up, know that a lot of doors will be closed but many will also be open in front of you, just endure the process right through. *From good support come great ideas*, more clients, and new employees, if you learn how to build up the best promotion with word a mouth. Then you won't miss out any opportunity to meet new people who can help you, just make sure you are available to return the favor someday.

Be in demand and pass on your skills:

Research has shown that the highest-paid individuals are usually the ones who have a particular education or skill set in areas that businesses or other people need the most. Rather than seeking after a whole bunch with just the common knowledge, they filter out the best. Become that educated individual who has a considerable amount of insight and knowledge about your field that you are sought-after constantly. The more extensive and honed your skill set becomes, the better the opportunities you will have to move ahead into your career. You can even increase these skills through your own experiences and from the things you have learnt. Then teach others how they can create or master their own. But you must explain why it is important to adopt these life-long learning habits, so they can also pass it on and continue the process.

Promote growth and this will attract people:

First you must become effective in managing any content, idea, or services you offer. When consumers or followers see how well you can do this, it will commission more opportunities to come your way. For example, let's pretend you sold over a US$100,000 in products in the past six months, your boss or business partners will realize your efforts and most likely reward you. Even if it is with an online store, a private practice or a social media account, the business will grow to be so successful it has more clients and buyers with the same effect. Your options thereafter will be so magnanimous that when they start pouring in from all over, you won't even believe it.

Encourage good working habits:

An influential person encourages good working habits that will improve their business or their partners to be more productive; it's about setting priorities and being proactive at the same time. Boost your achievement capacity that your family, friends, followers, and coworkers can put in their efforts to achieve more from their ROTI (return on time invested) in a shorter period. When everyone is organized and taking initiative on the tasks or the projects given out individually, it then increases their reward and their growth.

Reflect a productive mental attitude:

You have the power to choose a positive mental attitude over the negative no matter what you're going through. If you take it as a responsibility to look at the positive side of things, then you will manage to move on faster in life even from any situation. It might sound very horrid to some people, but it is not that hard if you try it, everything we do and don't do, comes down to a "choice." So, a positive mental attitude will benefit you personally and professionally in your everyday life, no matter what lifestyle you decide to live.

Personify a positive image:

We must dress for success. Yes, it is true that people are led by appearances unfortunately and it's no surprise that they tend to criticize and judge you by the way you look. I try not to do it often; but there is no shame in the game, because its human nature. I definitely believe it is worth some time to invest in and find the right resources to present yourself to others that will create that positive image or look, so you can stand out exquisitely to the world.

Birth creativity in people:

Creativity is a great way to start moving ahead in life, a lot of people who have influence can also help others to create new ideas, products, and even new services. This is something that you must work at continually to bring about your dreams and goals to fruition sooner than later. Keep in mind that it can sometimes take that one great idea to "create wealth." And imagine if you have other great ideas that some people have not heard of, just waiting to be delivered to improve their lives.

Build a strong character:

Influence comes with respect, followed by trust, and then builds a strong foundation for your personal and professional relationships. Being self-disciplined and honest will open a world of opportunities for you because my mentor once told me, *"Your private life will not be private once your life is in the eyes of the public."* So, when people know you are a person of integrity, they're more likely to trust you and believe in you. Hence why you must live that life you wish to lead every day.

WHAT TO DO IF YOU HAVE A GOOD STARTING POINT?

Studies have shown that people who are exposed to privilege and luck in life usually are not even conscious of it. They attribute their success much more to themselves rather than the circumstances (or the power) which allowed it *(Daniel 2:21 KJV).* If your success becomes so massive in life, do not embellish yourselves to appear too cocky and conceited as times passes. This way you will never abuse your power or your influence.

If you had a good starting point in life, then be very grateful and appreciate it. Not too many people were born into a well-developed state or a prosperous country. Nor did they have any loving and supportive parents, much more to get a good education with it. If you were raised in a supportive environment, with a lofty financial backing, then be thankful and never take it for granted. The next step is what will you do with all this privilege that was given to you? The reason for having a good starting point financially is not that you can lay back and enjoy it more than others, but that this privilege was entrusted to you so you could achieve more to benefit others in a particular way. (Proverbs 11:25 KJV)

When you've been placed in a position of influence, it is not by accident but more of a choice, because it was meant to create more value and to help the world to become a better place. So, you shouldn't waste any of your talents or leverages. If you *luxuriate* your fame for too long, this will slowly put you back in a lower starting position. By fooling around and not taking life seriously, you will sooner or later come face to face with the platitude that "wealth or success doesn't last for more than a few generations." No matter how many times you succeed and win at anything, celebrate it but stay humble and never get too pompous. (Luke 14:11 KJV)

In the business world a lot of people including entrepreneurs use the same winning formula over and over. So, pay attention to those who remain humble and wealthy. Do not become overly confident that you don't see the changes in the environment or the circumstances that occurs.

You can always find thousands of cases in which a businessperson gambles everything they have after a few success stories, but consequently loses everything thereafter. So don't let the success cloud your judgment at times. Always reflect on your actions regularly, so you can catch yourself before you act.

*This new generation is obsessed with looking successful, instead of actually being successful —**Kanye West, Ye** (American musician)*

Chapter 9

Why Should I Start a Business?

*Don't commit to anything unless you're going to do it — **Ralton Thompson***

Starting a business today is way easier than it was many years ago; and it may appear scary if you've never done it before, but this investment will help you to sustain any current economic downturn or recessions to come. There are roughly over 30 million small businesses in the United States, according to the Small Business Administration's and not all are all active and functioning businesses. These same small businesses comprise 99% of all U.S. businesses, which makes up the backbone of the U.S. economy. So, nearly half of all Americans and residents make up 48% of who are employed by small businesses. And to break this down, you would be adding yourself to the long list of business owners that will be very impactful in many ways.

The population in the U.S is estimated to be over 300 million people to date. So, there are more reasons to find solutions to all the problems that America has, let alone all the other problems in the world. And with today's high cost of living, overprice increase on commodities, services and new technology being introduced, we need a stable source of both passive and active income now more than ever.

When starting a business there's a lot to think about, generally if you don't know nothing about business. So, fear and doubt usually cloud our minds constantly. Then we have those who find it easier, and they go on to setup business (or businesses).

But what is important is to do the research to get all the necessary information needed. Then seek out legal or professional guidance to help you build up more confidence. Just put yourself in the position like I did, once I decide that I am going to do something, I am going to do it! The results are what I am looking for, so it's either it's going to work, or it won't.

You may be saying I don't have enough time, well, all of us do, you just have to "make" it and break it down into 168 hours per week.

That is **40hrs** at your job or the work you do
7hrs doing recreational activities or less
56hrs of sleeping or resting
And **65hrs** remaining to do anything productive. So, stop wasting time and start doing.

There are people who have started their business years ago, with no business plan, some didn't have access to computers, or any information on the latest research to know what is going on in the markets. They were risk-takers, but are you one of them? The future always involves taking risks. Even when you have everything planned out, you just have to go for it.

A lot of the resources we have in the United States come from other parts of the world. So even if you are in Africa, the Caribbean, South America, or Asia you can start a business successfully, if you go about it the right way. Listen, I was constantly being reminded that I was broke every time I saw the price for something extravagant that I wanted, and I complained it was too expensive, but it was not.

All of us just want that satisfaction of not worrying where the next dollar is coming from, even if we spend it on certain items. In that moment I realized I had to start my own business for a number of reasons, which then yielded me profits and other benefits over time. Maybe these reasons will give you the push you need to start today.

Note: *Every problem in life is a business, use your gifts or talents to solve them, and this will be your work, not your job...* — **Ralton Thompson**

1. Providing for your family

A solid reason to start a business comes down to supporting your family. In life, family always comes first. It's not just about putting food on the table it's also about making sure your family has money to create special memories together. Like vacations, weekend getaways at the cottage or the cabin, maybe trips to the amusement park, or a special party for your children.

It's important to make sure your children are set up to be successful, giving them the best tutors, you can afford, being active in sports or dance classes, and buying those informational books, plus more.

2. A pathway to freedom

If you ask people why they started a business, experiencing freedom would be on top of their list. From taking vacations when you want, to waking up at any hour of the day, running a business allows absolute "control" over how to schedule your day, your breaks, who you spend time with, what days you work, and much more. The biggest reason for starting a business is to have your life under control. You can help provide a higher quality of life for your family that a 9 to 5 job will never match.

3. Create a product or service people need

Every product or service has a purpose; you must decide what benefit this will bring to the consumers. I created features in my business that will communicate the capability of the product and service which makes it unique and set apart from my competition. You want to create products or services with features that your customers perceive as valuable to them. By highlighting benefits in marketing and sales efforts, you'll increase your sales and profitability.

It's important to remember that customers buy products and services because they want you to solve a problem or meet their needs. You are in the business of delivering solutions and satisfying needs, or they won't be successful.

4. Pursuing Your Passions

If you have a natural love and talent for music, then do it. Another way to pursue your passion(s) is through entrepreneurship. You can spend time on a hobby or even apply your gifts and talents to develop a new service, maybe a product as mentioned earlier, this can naturally transition into a business. You never know what impact your passions can have on the wider world.

*"I pay no attention whatever to anybody's praise or blame. I simply follow my own feelings."— **Wolfgang Amadeus Mozart** (Composer)*

5. Build a network with others who have similar interests

I started a non-profit organization so I could give back to the communities both locally and overseas, mainly in the under-privilege areas that lack of certain support from the Government and other business entities.

Even though it became an effective marketing method for raising awareness to find others, I did it because I could give back and find more people who wanted to support the movement. From this you can get referrals and introductions, some can be either face-to-face, maybe at social gatherings or even from business meetings. Other contacts could come through social media and unusual business networking. But you must first find a "su-i generis" way of building a business around good support.

6. You can do things better

If you believe there is a difference you can add to the world, I say go for it. Answer this question, is there any existing company or business doing everything right in this world? and name one without fault? We can always find more innovative ways and methods to conduct business, right? And this way they can increase efficiency and productivity to others. The simple fact still remains that we haven't invented everything yet and we can still improve the world, hence it is another reason to start a business.

Think about your life every day. Is everything perfect in it? No, so what changes do you think will improve it? We all sit back and wish there was some way to beat or fix these issues we have, and there is, but we usually complain, and hope that someday it gets better. But what if that change today is you? Or what if your contribution can make a difference? I believe each stumbling block or obstacle in your path could be a business opportunity.

When you have a problem in life, ask yourself: Does a good solution already exist out there? If not, how many other people have this problem? If they don't have one, consider starting a business based around a solution to your problem or theirs.

"No action is too small when it comes to changing the world... I'm inspired every time I meet an entrepreneur who is succeeding against all odds." — **Cyril Ramaphosa** (South African businessman)

7. You Can Create Jobs

One of the major advantages and noblest thing you could ever do is to start a business or a company that can hire employees to work. You would have created an opportunity for someone else to feed their family, get training, and learn new skills. When you first start off your business it's going to be small, but oftentimes it is the same small businesses that creates the most jobs and then grow bigger.

As the owner of the company, you can treat your employees well, create a resplendent company culture, and also make people feel highly involved in a business that is lionized and highly influential. Here you can be both the boss you wish you had or even emulated and the mentor you wanted others to learn from. I have witness myself accomplishing tough things, when no one else believed in me or think I could do it; and it gives off that joy of fulfillment when I do. Success will always increase your *self-worth* and allow you to take the credit for anything meaningful you do, as long as you can achieve it then you will have it.

Starting a business is no small venture, especially when it becomes successful after taking off. For many of you on this path, it will take long hours, failures, financial losses, rejection and working harder to move upwards through the ranks of competition. But that comes with the territory; real entrepreneurs don't retract their efforts or hold back from a challenge, they aim higher to do bigger things, so keep that same energy, and do it every day.

DO NOT BE DISCOURAGED IF YOUR REASONS TO START A BUSINESS IS NOT MENTIONED

The list is only a few of the reasons of why it is important to start a business, and I know fear can be a big enough reason that hinders you from moving forward, because oftentimes we believe we are not good enough.

A lot of people get hampered from starting a business, because of their age, the lack of the education or they have limited skills. The biggest blocker most times is lack of financial support, but I didn't make that stop me, even when my credit was bad, I still pursued it.

The way I keep going is not by looking at my restrictions, even when the doctors deemed me as *chronically ill.* I went after it because I know I'm going to make a difference in the process. Doubt and fear usually hold us back because we are waiting for the perfect conditions to launch our business; but it's never going come like that.

Every business owner works through layers of different experiences, and those experiences are chances that never gets manifested, if the person continues to be scared to start their own business, then it won't happen. I can throw in a lot of scenarios or data at you, about what researchers say and why people have started their business. But there's more to it than that, starting a business most times is personal to you, than it is to someone else. Some business will grow huge success, and some will stay small. Some can become a new profession, and some may remain a side hustle.

Most importantly you will need a business plan, for this will be the road map to guide your ideas and get you results along the way. Rather than putting yourself in a position where you may have to stop and ask for directions, start with one first. A lot of entrepreneurs will use a business plan to follow through because it will show you the bigger picture, to plan ahead, make important decisions, and improve your chance of success.

I believe most individual have the diversity to push through entrepreneurial boundaries. While others will work tacitly to do conventional things that will still make a difference in the world. In the end, you have to choose to do it or not to do anything at all, because I know some things are just not for everyone.

"You can only become truly accomplished at something you love. Don't make money your goal. Instead, pursue the things you love doing, and then do them so well that people can't take their eyes off you." **— Maya Angelou** *(American poet)*

Chapter 10

Money Habits That Will Help You Become Wealthy

"Every accomplishment starts with the decision to try."
— *John F. Kennedy (35th U.S. President)*

Not everyone is dreaming about building wealth, but everybody is dreaming about being rich. If you decide, in this chapter are some habits you need to start practicing that will get you there quickly.

In today's world, technology can help you to automate a lot of these habits but depending on technology is not always the best resort. This can reduce your self-dependency to the amount of personal discipline you apply to the process. We need discipline in the beginning, and we must commit while forming these habits. But I have noticed once we established them, we can continue these habits without thinking about it in the long run.

All accomplishments will not always happen overnight, so I don't expect all these habits that I have listed to be implemented all at once. So, picking the ones manageable first, mastering it, and then choosing the others to tackle is a good start. Each good money habit you master, can build up more momentum on your road to wealth, just stay on track and remain committed.

1. Budget is mandatory

On paper you want to create a new budget from scratch, you must design it to maximize your entire savings, because without a budget, it's hard to stay financially stable. It doesn't matter how much you earn if you keep spending every penny.

At the end of the year, if a person who earns US$1 million spends all their money and another who earns US$50,000 does the same, then their net worth is $0. Because both spent all their income and didn't manage it properly.

The greatest opportunities for savings come from your largest expenses: such as housing, transportation, and food. These three categories alone combine to make up nearly two-thirds of the average household expenditure. I would suggest start by cutting any additional expenses which often requires a major life adjustment.

While you work towards your ideal budget, start with intermediate steps such as getting rid of some entertainment subscriptions, canceling unused memberships or anything you rarely use that don't excite you.

2. Automate Expenses (including Savings)

If you have to remember to pay all your bills every month, eventually you will forget a few and you do not want to have a late payment history. Good budgets usually start with your saving amount as your highest priority. Set a percentage rate from your after-tax income as a desired savings amount, and set up automated recurring transfers to your savings account or brokerage account if you have one, etc.

Normally I keep a weekly reminder of what scheduled transfers should take place every time I get a paycheck from a client or customer. But don't stop there. Set up automatic payments for your mortgage or rent, your car payment, utility bills, credit card payments, and every other bill in your monthly budget. The more you can automate the better the results, which will discipline your habits.

3. Restrict Your Spending as You Earn More

When the average person gets a raise, they immediately find a way to spend it. Unfortunately, this ruins them financially, many of us run to purchase a luxury car, or a larger home, even splurging it on unnecessary items that don't give us any "return in value," this habit just leads us down a path of financial bondage. So, no matter how much money you earn, you can never actually get rich or become wealthy by spending it all the time.

Save at least 25-30% of your income every month

The first step to becoming wealthy is to save a portion of your paycheck every month when starting out with nothing, no matter how much or how little you make. Always set aside at least 25% to 30% every month, it can be more, but never less.

This effect I call a **saving stimulus.** And if you want to build wealth overtime, you need to fight constantly and consistently to get to it.

The battles we fight to save money are the variables that keep coming at us all the time, but you can't allow your expenses to keep creeping up on you, especially as you earn more money. Set a percentage of any future pay raises that you will let yourself spend. For example, if you spend 25% of a pay raise and you get an extra US$500 per month. Then change your budget to spend only US$125 from that and stick to it.

The key is to always remain "committed" to your savings amount if you want to build wealth faster. Spending less helps and serves as a great defense. But it also helps you to earn more money and to play offense. Your goal in building wealth is to grow the gap between what you earn and what you spend. It's that simple!

4. Pay off All Unsecured Personal Debts in Full, every month if possible

Prioritize your high-interest unsecured debts first, these include your credit cards, personal loans and student loans as well. You already know how to automate your bill payments from the first lesson. Now pick your smallest debt whether by balance or the highest-interest fee you have and pay down as much every month on each debt. When you pay one debt in full then move to the next, until you have no more unsecured *personal* debt.

Note that "unsecured" refers to the debt not being attached to your home or car. Secured debt, such as mortgages and auto loans, tend to cost less in interest sometimes and those can stay further down on the priority list. If you want to be wealthy, focus on paying off your personal debts. I personally learned how to leverage business debts after making drastic financial changes, because now it allows me to operate differently, and I am able to create more assets protection that I couldn't do on the personal side.

Next, find out if it makes sense to refinance your car loans, student loans or your mortgages for a better interest rate. You can also investigate things like student debt forgiveness because becoming debt-free is your number one priority! Don't be afraid to ask for anything, you can't accumulate wealth until you've eliminated the high interest "personal" debts.

Think about this: What's the point in investing money in the stock market or anywhere for a 10% average return, if you're paying 20% interest on credit cards or high debt loans? Far too many people carry unsecured debt everywhere they go. If you want to build wealth, you first need to build good credit habits anywhere in the world.

5. Improve & Track Your Credit

Make the extra effort to pay up all your personal bills on time for this will help improve your credibility anywhere. If you have a lot of personal credit cards, it is best to pay them off full each month, so it doesn't affect your credit rating. As you pay off these credit cards, don't close them even if you don't use them often. The credit reporting agencies look on your credit history on a whole, along with the average age of your accounts and how long you have been holding these accounts. Learn more about credit reporting so you can increase your scores faster and remove negative items. There are companies out there who report every bad debt you have to keep you down in a hole, and lenders will use this information to give you the highest interest rates each time you apply for a loan or lines of credit.

6. Start a Work Lifestyle

There are many people today that get stuck in a job or a career out of convenience, only so they can provide for themselves or their families. But most of these jobs don't always give them the lifestyle they desperately want outside of work. Don't just focus on earning more money. Start writing out the life you want in your career, your relationships and your business, then take those steps to make it happen.

This might be going back to school for additional certification or training, sacrificing one job for another, or even volunteering at the shelters to help the poor and needy. What's the point of living a lie at work and no life at home? Set the goals or the expectations of yourself and not of others. Pursue whatever lifestyle that's unique to you, and make sure your career goals align with your greater life purpose that is meaningful and noble.

7. Saying No to the Wrong Money

The wrong money will keep you in commonplaceness. It will make you unhappy, tired, and resentful, this I have experienced over the years. A lot of people are making the "wrong" money moves right now.

I can recall many opportunities where I have taken the wrong money, and couldn't keep it, oh yes; it was a high-paying gig too that would ultimately become a burden later on, taking away from me what truly matters.

The wrong money can be any money earned while doing jobs that are irrelevant to your true purpose. And the wrong money is abundant everywhere and easy to come by. Ironically, it becomes more "teeming" when you finally start taking the right steps towards what really matters and doing the right thing. Believe me the temptation is real.

"People are unhappy in large part because they are confused about what is valuable."
— **William Irvine** *(Philosopher)*

8. Never Lose Interest or Stop Learning

There is a saying that goes: Leaders are readers" and I believe it is true, because they never stop learning; growing, or challenging themselves. In *Revelation 1:3* KJV bible it says, **"Blessed is he that readeth, and they that hear the words of this prophecy, and keep those things which are written therein: for the time is at hand."** This means we must always stay in touch with *God's* teachings and what's happening around us for own benefit.

Keeping current with the right events or trends, particularly in your career or your chosen field, because it's vital for your continued success. For example, I spend 30-40 minutes daily browsing through the most recent online news, market updates or simply the weather changes after eating breakfast most mornings.

Then 20-25 minutes browsing through social media to see what is happening around the world. But continuous learning also means taking a long view of life by nurturing yourself personally and professionally through reading books, blogs, listening to audios, podcasts, and watching video training courses. Only you know what will drive the most growth in your own career or personal life. Whatever you choose, know that the wealthiest and happiest people maintain a habit of constant growth.

9. Explore Additional Income Sources

In today's fast lane job economy, you can earn extra money immediately with a side hustle. This could include a *low-skill* and potentially relaxing gig such as a delivery job and a landscaper or a *high-skill* job such as a freelancer working as a photographer, writer, or a public relations specialist.

Think about entering that entrepreneurial mindset and start a side business while working a full-time job. Everyone should understand it's not about working harder, it's about "working smarter," even if it is not that hard, get in the habit of working those long hours for a while because it will pay off in the end.

Growing up I saw my father working for the Police Department in Jamaica and having a restaurant as his side business. What you do outside your regular work hours will determine your success. Whether it's generating additional income, starting a business, or working up the corporate ladder, these efforts all serve a single purpose of creating wealth for a long term.

10. Create Multiple Passive Income Streams

50% of the acclaimed self-made millionaires that I have studied all had at least three streams of income, some from one business and other from multiple businesses. 30% had four streams and 20% had five or more streams of income that they created before making their first million or more. You want to be able to make money while you're sleeping, and who doesn't? I started out earning extra money by reselling products and buying and selling used cars, then I went into real estate ventures. Eventually the plan was to have enough passive income to cover all my expenses and give me that financial independence to work when and where I wanted to anytime.

When you build passive income, you reduce your dependence on your job and give yourself the freedom to explore more options and take risks on new ideas.

11. Invest Regularly & Wisely

Many new investors can find themselves intimidated when it comes to investing, whether it's with stocks, bonds, or some other asset investment. Nowadays you don't need to be rich to choose an asset to invest your money in, especially if you can learn how to manage your own portfolio. You must however seek out the right avenues where you can get your money managed properly. But ensure you monitor your investments based on your goals and the risk tolerance you can handle. Always keep your eyes on everything, from transferring money from one account to the next, and when purchasing investments or balancing your portfolio. And this goes for any brokerage that also invests money on your behalf.

I don't trust everyone with money and because these transactions happen on a regular basis, I try to eliminate my emotions from all investments, so I can reduce the risk as an investor.

Pro tip: If you're not comfortable with your current brokerage or firm then consider opening a new account with another broker, never settle for a second-rated service. Always try to stay with the best regardless of the affiliation.

Saving money is all well and good, but what to do with it after?

You invest it. Author of "Rich Dad, Poor Dad," Robert Kiyosaki said "The rich don't work for money. Their money works for them." Money can work for you through two systems: long-term growth and passive income. And both will help your wealth and your money compound over time. So be patient!

12. Surround Yourself with Like-Minded People

There is an old saying that goes "you are the average of the five people you spend the most of your time with," and a lot of people will agree with this. If you want to build a business or even yourself, you should spend more time with those who own businesses. If you want to reach financial independence at a young age then hang out with others who share the same goal, I can assure you that if they're real productive friends they shouldn't be proposing you go out for US$300 dinners every weekend.

To reiterate when I say, "like-minded people," I don't mean people who share your political beliefs or educational background, even shopping habits or those who never challenge you to do things different. I mean people who share your long-term financial and lifestyle goals.

Note: Long-term goals require determined commitment, and this discipline sometimes gets challenge by outside influence. So, when this happens, it is necessary to have people who share your vision to build you back up. And along the way they also can reveal new ideas that will help you achieve your goals even faster.

13. Align Your Financial Vision with Your partner

Oftentimes a lot of couples enter a relationship with their own financial goals in mind. But end up ditching these goals after they get married. Merging your business ideas with a partner should not be swept under the rug. Instead, work together to bring alive each other's goals simultaneously to keep both you and your spouse or partner happy and on the same page financially.

Before you start budgeting for your own financial goals, consider the following steps to get your partner or spouse on board as well.

Communicate each goal to one another

Choose a time to meet and discuss your financial goals. When you meet, both you and your spouse or partner should bring your own list of goals to the table for discussion. The list can include:

- Short-term goals (achievable in one year or less)

- Medium-term goals (achievable in one to three years)

- Long-term goals (achievable in more than five years)

The aim also is to see if you and your partner or spouse are *"financially compatible"* and will both last through the relationship for that season. It is very critical to grow in all aspect of your lives, so the list must be shared with one another, be flexible and understanding as you go through them.

Setting financial goals as a couple or with a business partner doesn't mean you have to give up on all your personal goals. But sharing the vision of goals will make them come a reality by helping each other. This can help each one to feel equal in the process.

Make the financial goals actionable and attainable

When choosing to share your individual goals, you need to make them realistic and actionable. Together, you should discuss the reality of what it takes to meet these goals.

This helps remove doubts out of the equation." For example, anyone could dream of making US$1 million in the next two years, but if you are only making US$70,000 per year or less, it's highly unlikely if you have no way to increase your earning power. Again, overnight success is not what you see on T.V.

Create a Plan

When you create your list of goals, it's time to work on them. But together, you must prioritize the goals within each category (short-term, medium-term, and long-term). Remember it is necessary to come to an agreement throughout the process, while prioritizing both shared and individualistic goals.

Next, you need to look closely at your budget; this is something I will continue to reinforce. Pay attention to your *net* household income and your business, after that minus your total monthly expenses (e.g., rent or mortgage, car payments, utilities, groceries, etc.). These are non-negotiable expenses that should come first. You must employ a strategy to reach your financial goals, and this will begin with the money you have left after covering all the necessities.

To operate efficiently you must have peace of mind in your home and in your business. Together you and your partner should decide how to use the remaining money between the personal spending needs and your goals.

Once you have the budget amount for your goals, look at each other goals separately on your list, and break them down into specific steps. For example, if you want a 30% down payment on a house or condo, in the next two years or less, calculate how much you will need to save per month. Maybe your business needs new equipment or furniture; calculate what spending expenses must be cut to save towards this. Check if it fits into your budget. Does it align with your other short-term and mid-term goals? If it's unrealistic, then go back to the drawing board so you can make it work.

Set up regular check-ins or meetings

Keep each other accountable to bring about these goals, for it will help you to stay on track. It is also a great reminder to stay flexible. So set up regular "meetings" to see where you stand. At each meeting, discuss the progress you've made and reassess your financial situation each time, has anything change? such as your personal or household expenses or maybe your income?

I usually set up rewards to celebrate my successes. Each time someone meets a milestone, you can reward them, even yourself. Showing one another the simple joy, you have in achieving a goal, can help them stay motivated while moving forward.

Stay flexible

Remember that life happens. Don't get upset if you experience a setback; just keep the lines of communication open. Stay flexible throughout the process so you can see the bigger picture. For example, if you or your spouse should lose your job, you may have to delay your plans for a while until you get back on your feet. Also revisit your goals often. You may achieve some of your goals sooner, while some don't fit on your list any longer. An example could be you had saved up enough money in an emergency account to the point where you don't need to work extra days, well stop! so you can move on to the next goal.

Support each other financial goals

Creating shared goals with your partner will help you stay connected and can prevent unnecessary fights about money. If both partners are on the same page, you can achieve individual goals by just supporting each other through the process.

14. Where should I put my money during a recession or a pandemic?

In uncertain times, it's important to ensure your money is *safe*. I know many individuals are missing out on opportunities to safeguard their money even on guaranteed returns as their money grows weaker in a bank.

You must rest easy when putting your money in a secured investment that can be liquidated quickly if needs be, like most Americans do, they put their money where it is FDIC insured. Which means Federal Deposit Insurance Corporation (FDIC) started by the U.S Congress to maintain stability and public confidence in the nation's financial system.

I personally don't keep my money in the bank because the standard insurance amount is ONLY US$250,000 per depositor, per insured bank, and for each account type. So, if I lose more than US$300,000 because of theft, fraudulent activities, or any inconvenient circumstances I'm not getting it back. I look for more assets to buy when I saved up enough money. However, I cannot make suggestions for your investments, only directions. You must decide if the assets you choose will give you ten times (10x) more interest or ten times (10x) more returns than the national average allocated in your country or here in the U.S.

15. Volunteering and giving to Charity

It's nothing new that the wealthy gives a lot of money to charity, and millions of Americans will also open their pockets for a good cause during the seasons, but the rich will give their charitable donations differently than the average person. Records have indicated that a smaller percentage of the wealthier donors gave to charity because they were motivated for tax benefits and a larger percentage said they gave for other reasons. While the remainder gave because they believe their gift or contribution can make a difference in the world.

Contributions to nonprofits are generally tax deductible, which means you can lower your annual tax expense. Although you will have to itemize the donations to get a tax break, some critics will argue that the wealthier individuals get more tax benefits from that part of the law because they give more, and it so happens to be true in most countries.

I have done some research and found out that an average of 20 - 30% of self-made millionaires usually volunteer their time, somewhere between three to six hours each month by giving back to the community. My first personal experience in giving to charity was back in 2018, when I donated to a popular non-profit organization who in turn gave me a free vacation to visit any 50 State, so I chose San Diego, in California. This for me was a humbling experience.

Studies by Healthcare companies and volunteer programs show that at least 71% of those who had volunteered in charity events or other recreational functions felt healthier after participating. Then 64% reported lowered stress levels, and 93% felt generally happier. According to other research companies' more evidence was presented to suggest volunteering helps you live longer when you are always active. To make an even more powerful revelation, studies have shown that wealthy individuals and people who are becoming successful that gives more generously and willing, tend to earn more money over time.

I believe if we want to achieve anything great in our lives, we must be ready to accept a lot of discomfort, whether it's with our jobs, our finances or in our relationships, because all of that is only temporary. A lot of people have settled for the ordinary, even for the things that is just "good enough," and nothing is wrong. You can always continue with the same lifestyle, the same spending habits, and the same hoarding without giving anything away. But I rather be ready to leave behind what was comfortable for something greater. The ultimate sacrifice will show the changes necessary to gain what is truly magnificent in the future.

Chapter 11

Make Your Choice to Be Rich or to Become Wealthy

"If my mind can conceive it, and my heart can believe it, then I can achieve it."
— ***Muhammad Ali*** *(Professional boxer)*

I have often thought over the years what is the difference between the rich and the wealthy? If so, what is it? And how do I become wealthy? Or is it better to just be rich?

Let's go back in time to what the meaning of wealth was. So, the word 'wealth' comes from the old English word 'weal', which originally meant 'welfare, prosperity and wellbeing'. Weal was then merged with "well" to give the Middle English word 'welthe' relating to the older word 'well', meaning 'in good health, or happiness' which formed what we called today **'wealth'** around 1250 AD.

By 1430 it was believed to have been finalized around the idea of "riches and material prosperity," leaving the older usage of wellbeing and health behind today.

The difference Between the Rich & the Wealthy

I believe there is a big disparity between being rich and being wealthy. When I think about someone who is rich, I think of someone with a lot of money in their bank accounts. Typically, they act quite pretentious with their money, and I know a lot of people will argue this. But most are associated with driving expensive cars, living in luxurious homes or condos, or wearing designer clothes and the list goes on.

Rich people may come into their money in a number of ways. From an inheritance through their family, a business or businesses, insurance policies, and more popularly winning the lottery and so forth. They may also earn it in a few short years as professional sports players or entertainers. Some might have been inventors of new products or ideas worth millions of dollars.

Does this also describe a wealthy person and is there unquestionably a difference? Well, yes, I believe there is a major difference between the rich and the wealthy.

I believe time makes the difference. How long does money last anyone though? Will it be gone once the person's earning capabilities are gone? Will it be passed on to the future generations? Only wealth can do that and it's not how much money you possess "presently." In other words, a wealthy person will always be wealthy, whereas a rich person will only be for a period a time, until their money is used up. To simply put it, a rich person doesn't necessarily have to have millions of dollars neither does a wealthy person, *it's their possessions that as the sustainability through the test of time* and *not the amount of money* they have which is the difference.

Jamaican Reggae Icon Bob Marley once asked an interviewer, "How much is a lot of money to you? But he couldn't answer, he then asked Bob, "if he is a rich man and does he have a lot of possessions, a lot of money in the bank?" But Bob replied smartly and said, "do possessions make you rich?" I don't have that type of richness; my richness is life forever!" Although Bob Marley could buy anything he desired at that time, money never represented riches to him. Today his music and his legacy are worth hundreds of millions of U.S. dollars.

Think about all the people in our history who others have considered to be wealthy? This can be where you live now or the individuals you know of in other countries. You will begin to see what I mean. These billionaire families have decades of wealth passed down, from the Walton Family, who are owners of Walmart, then the Saudi Royal Family, who made generational fortunes from the oil industries. Not to exclude the Rothschild, the Carnegies and the Rockefellers who are all wealthy families. Their wealth has lasted multiple generations. Why is this? What makes them so different from the lottery winners or some professional athletes who only have money for a short period of time and then they lose it?

Another major difference between the rich and the wealthy is *knowledge*. Wealthy people know how to make and keep money. But most rich people only have money. Once you know how to make money, you can build sustainable wealth anywhere. The money never stops coming in, even if you had loss a fortune you never panic, because you can make it again. And starting over is easier with that knowledge and experience you have gathered over time.

Think about the entertainer and businessman Curtis "50 Cent" Jackson. Years ago, he was deeply in debt and filed for Bankruptcy with an estimated debt of US$36 million and assets less than US$20 million. But oddly, he didn't change his spending habits. Jackson nearly got in more trouble for an internet post when he posed up with stacks of cash on social media. The judge questioned if he was really declaring all his assets, but Jackson said, "he was merely living up to his perceived image," and why not? A lot of people pretend to be rich on T.V. or social media, just to win the hearts and soul of others, so they can buy what they are selling. So, Curtis "50 Cent" Jackson had first-hand knowledge on how to make money and keep it and he can be considered a wealthy individual today.

There are many examples of people who obtained their wealth through knowledge, and they are others who do value knowledge over money. The most renowned one was King Solomon. He had great wealth beyond measure and supernatural wisdom. When he first became king, the biblical scriptures said he went to Gibeon to sacrifice to the *Most High God,* and later appeared to Solomon in a dream asking what he wanted. Solomon then asked for "wisdom and understanding" to rule over the Israelites, unlike the Kings before him it pleased *God* so much, that he added more than what Solomon had asked for, which was honor and riches. Throughout Solomon's writings and in is books, he mentioned wisdom and knowledge as the two most important gifts to ask from *God*.

When we think of someone being rich versus wealthy, we might think it's the same thing, but it's not. For some reason, the words rich and wealthy are often interchangeably used to describe the same thing. Wisdom and knowledge can create great wealth for anyone who desires it, but the knowledge needs to come first. Otherwise, if you do happen to get rich, and it's by chance likely the money will not last very long.

Money and Relationships

The Lifestyle of the Rich

The rich come in many forms than the average person, but you can only tell the difference over time and from their actions, if you pay attention long enough. A median is set in every country that dictates what category of earnings everyone falls in.

So, it doesn't matter how much money you have, if your expenses are higher than your income, this will lead to debt, and it is not something good for anyone to aspire to. Plenty of celebrities have gone broke because of their rich lifestyles and habits.

Nicolas Cage was one of Hollywood's biggest stars earning around US$40 million in 2009 but was also one of its biggest spenders. Cage purchased many homes, sport cars, and rare artifacts. However, in 2015, reports started to come out about how he blew his US$150 million fortune from 1996 to 2011.

The Internal Revenue Service had tax liens on his properties and then Cage had to pay out more than US$6 million for noncompliance obligations owed on a 2007 tax bill. His precarious financial situation led him to sell many of his personal belongings, including items of unique value and peculiar scarcity.

Another entertainer, MC Hammer which despite his hit "U Can't Touch This," had to file for bankruptcy in 1996. At one point he had US$30 million in the bank, a US$1 million house with 200 staff members, and a horse stable with 19 racehorses. But all those expenses and misuse spending including several lawsuits landed him in a US$13 million in debt.

Let's go back into history to also give an example where Civil War General Ulysses S. Grant a U.S president went broke after leaving the White House, it is tough to imagine that right? But that's what happened to the 18th U.S president. Grant became a partner in a financial firm called *Grant and Ward*, but Ferdinand Ward embezzled investors' money, leaving the firm and Grant had to filed for bankruptcy in 1884. He was receiving a military pension, but it wasn't enough, due to his long suffering from throat cancer. To make money, Grant asked author *Mark Twain* to publish his memoirs, but he died before he could make any money from his life story.

What does it mean to be wealthy?

To explain wealth, it is not about having all this exuberant amount of money to meet all your needs, but it is ability to *afford* not to work if you don't have to. It's also about accruing valued assets and making your money work for you while building up a considerable net worth.

A lot of wealthy people don't necessarily buy the latest clothes, techs or luxury cars or throw these lavish parties as people think. What they do is buy a lot of money producing assets, such as real estate and other investments. For example, if you purchase a rental property maybe in the United States or in another country and get it rented out or leased. Say the monthly income can give you an estimated return of two-three times **(2-3X)** the amount of the mortgage expenses, and you have a consistent monthly savings of eight to ten times **(8-10X)** your income after personal expenses. Then your net worth begins to grow in an investment stream, which now can afford you certain luxuries.

The wealthiest Americans are usually business owners, investors, and bankers. The famous Warren Buffet who is worth billions of dollars today, his considered to be a frugal business billionaire. Despite his massive wealth it is said that he still lives in his first home he bought in 1958 for around US$31,500. He purchased other properties even a vacation beach house in California for US$150,000 in 1971 but ended up selling it for US$7.5 million. Now that was a smart investment and look at his return? The problem with a lot of people these days is nobody wants to grow slow; a lot of people just want to be rich quick. And that's why a lot of people keep getting caught up in these get-rich quick schemes all over the world.

How can I become wealthy today?

If you want to become wealthy, there are a few things you can do to get started. In the previous chapters there are some tips and advice I mentioned to help you on the journey. I keep reinforcing this throughout the book because I believe constant reminders will bring forth action. So, pay attention to every bit of information and go back over it more than once if you need to. Follow these additional steps to eliminate any unnecessary debt and work very "smart" to develop the right mindset when it comes to amassing wealth.

Invest soon and as much as you can

One of the quickest ways to grow wealth is to "invest" it, yes invest it. We all know investing comes with its own risks, but there are plenty of options available out there. You can get investment advice from a professional broker, or just ensure you invest in goods or services other than the stock market that you understand.

Stocks might NOT work for everybody, so invest in what you understand. Try to learn as you go, and don't depend on others to know everything for you. No matter what you do, do something! You can also put your money in a high-yield savings account to accrue some interest until you're ready to invest it. Just make sure the money works for you.

Among the keys to growing wealth one must remain cautious in every spending and live within their means. In fact, you should spend just below your means to be exact, and many people might not want to do this, but remember it is ONLY temporary so you can invest that extra income.

Sometimes a partner might see you as being cheap, that's fine, and it might even cause a break in your relationship or business, but your goals are more important to you and your children, even to those who cannot fend for themselves.

SACRIFICES MUST ALWAYS BE MADE

This means resisting the urge to buy those designer clothes or purchasing the latest model cellphones when an older model will work just as good. Be smart about what you spend your money on, I encourage everyone only buy the things you do need, and not those things which will lose value quickly.

Think about your long-term financial goals and assets

Growing wealth is a long-term commitment; it's not something that just happens overnight. It took me years to buy my first property that is worth millions in my home country today, so it could take you years to build up your own wealth and that's okay. When things get tough and circumstances change for the worse, still remember your long-term goals and keep them. That is why you chose to become wealthy in the first place, don't get discourage no matter what may come at you.

Wealth is a mindset

Remember being wealthy doesn't start with a huge bank account full of money. It starts with the right mindset. So, focus on building yourself and becoming the best learner while investing in everything you can. If wealth is your endgame, then you need to always keep your long-term goals on the forefront of everything. Ask yourself do I want to retire early? Can I afford to travel the world anytime I want? Will I have enough generational income? When thinking about wealth just don't focus on your income for a year, focus on building your investments and assets that will outlast you.

A lot of people still believe there is some "secret formula" that enables others to become millionaires faster. Well, there isn't, it's a transitional process. If the average person knows how a typical millionaire became one, they would be surprised because there is more than one way. I had nothing in my background that qualified me to be a millionaire, but I knew I was going to be one. At first, I was just boxed in by the conventional myths I heard society talked about.

But let's start with this fact: If you believe you will NEVER become a millionaire, you will never be one. Becoming a millionaire requires the right *mindset*. And I had to change that in my own life, which took me years before I came close to being a millionaire. This can never happen until you change the way you think and any bad habits first. I quickly started finding ways of how to get possession of assets that was worth millions of dollars and when you can answer that carefully, you can go do it. But what would you do with US$1million right now if someone was to hand it to you? Could you turn that into US$3 million or even US$7 million in 90 days or less? Once you have answered that question too, you are transitioning into the **millionaire mindset.**

Many people are told different things about millionaires and sometimes it leads to misbelieve notions that are inconsistent and arguable. So I have put together a list of myths, that when you become a millionaire yourself you will educate them.

Myth 1: All Millionaires Only Inherit Their Money

A lot of millionaires solely just worked, they invest, and live within their means to generate their wealth, if you question it, some are simply accountants, lawyers, business managers, business owners, top executives, and regular people who just to work every day. Some walk pass you every day and you don't even know them.

According to Thomas J. Stanley's in his book, *The Millionaire Next Door: The Surprising Secrets of America's Wealthy,* he said only 20% of millionaires inherited their riches.

Myth 2: All Millionaires Feel Rich

From the outside looking in, you would think that most millionaires would feel rich and secure, right? But that's not so. Most millionaires worry about their retirement, even their mortgage just like the rest of us. Some millionaires do struggle with keeping their wealth and possessions too. In recent years there is a significant number of new millionaires and other people who have acquired their wealth in a shorter space of time, who might act rich on social media or in public. But in reality, they are really scared of losing all their money.

Myth 3: All Millionaires Don't Pay Taxes

It is estimated that most millionaires in the top 1% of earners, pay about 40% of all taxes. Believe it or not, the constant tax regulation changes will always affect these numbers anytime governments of different nations and countries change power. They tend to seek more revenue from every individual than those in the previous years, so think twice before accusing any millionaire of not paying taxes, they might *avoid* some taxes, BUT NOT ALL.

Myth 4: All Millionaires Hang Around the Golf Course All Day

Sometimes we see things portrayed on T.V. that deludes our thoughts and it's the same for most millionaires and how they are viewed. Some people think they don't do nothing else but hang around the golf course all day. Well, it's the opposite, cause only a small number of millionaires do this and some are usually retirees, the larger percentage amongst them do other things.

I know hearing this over and over might not be glamorous or fun to listen, but millionaires do go to work just like you and I; how else do we make money? Certainly not playing golf all day, I know some of them do, but not all can.

Myth 5: All Millionaires Are Elitist or Part of a Secret Society.

We've already established that most millionaires earned their money and not all of them inherit it. I bet you right now there are thousands of millionaires who drive Toyota's or Honda's you see every day, that have issues just like regular people and you can't even tell the difference. Millionaires do come in all manner and appearances, while some are truly elitist who belong to a secret group or an unnamed "autocrat" of people who run the world. Remember most are still normal individuals who successfully managed their money well. So don't get caught up with everything you see and hear out there.

Chapter 12

Success Advice for Modern Entrepreneurs

"Whosoever desires constant success must change his conduct with the times."
— **Niccolo Machiavelli** *(Italian philosopher, diplomat)*

Every single day, I know a lot of people get dozens of emails or social media advertisement from business services wanting to sell them something. You can see how the world has changed in doing business, and I am impressed with some of it, but not all of it. A company cannot be profitable unless it convinces its consumers or other businesses to try their products or services. So, the internet today is the best platform where businesses can advertise, connect with customers, and make sales. But there are so many people that quickly get seduce into buying bull crap services or products too. And it gets worse because some people end up becoming consumers, followers and clients of these Ponzi companies, influencers and fake internet gurus with nonsensical philosophies and virtual communities that allegedly teach them how to "hack" life.

I find it scarcely credible when I meet people who have been bouncing from one pyramid scheme to another, one online millionaire program to the next, and from one health product to another with little or no result. And still think they will soon find the right *"shortcut"* to hack certain life goals. This breaks my heart every time.

The only way to **"hack"** life is by working consistently and smartly to the end goal. Life was never meant to be "easy." If you are a shortcut kind of a person, unfortunately you will always end up trapped in these unethical practices that will lead to failure and humiliation.

110

If you really want to be successful at anything, you must develop a loving and respectful attitude towards life's challenges. You must keep improving your circle of friends to get ahead and build a good team.

Christian J. Ward, an American record producer who goes by the pseudonym *Hitmaka*, has done great work for music artiste such as Ariana Grande, Chris Brown, Nicki Minaj, T.I and many more entertainers. Hitmaka said "No matter how talented you are YOU CAN'T CHEAT THE GAME! I had to work for years with zero money, zero placements just "blind faith" that one day all the struggle was gone pay off and it did. As a growing entrepreneur you must study how to improve your life and others every day, and this will carry you into productive places.

Success Advice 101

1. Success requires hard work (not always physical) and high energy responses. But its courage, patience, and resilience, with teamwork that gives real results. An opportunity that promises to circumvent this process will likely be a scam.

2. If you are striving for the best work-life and it's something you desire dearly, then your business, your dreams and your goals will keep you from reaping other "fitful" rewards that come with experiencing everything.

3. Nothing is really *free* or guaranteed, so make it the norm to setup proper legal structures that is required to protect you, your business and your partner(s) before transacting or running any business operation.

4. *Pay* to get into rooms with more successful people than you. Most wealthy or successful individuals typically do business with other people they know or have been acquainted with through networking or by other credible means.

Just doing business with people you have never met, or you can't identify proof of their legitimacy with, is most likely a risky idea. Don't believe everything you see or hear on the T.V., radio or internet.

5. Most profitable businesses and some multifaceted deals still happens offline or in person. And there are still some businesses and investors whether online or offline that still depend on ground support and word of mouth, to get information out there so they can make money or let it work for them.

6. If you are getting letters or email invitation from strangers about fantastic business opportunities that seem very luring and enticing "usually" these are scams, so be very cautious about what they ask for in return sometimes.

7. **Overnight success and having it all is a "myth," it was never design like that, everything in life was meant to be shared, even the time we get to give each other.**

8. Pay close attention to these online videos and pictures of attractive people making promises. A lot will share shortcuts on how to be rich while driving luxury cars, but this is not enough evidence to show you the "right path to success." Just remember it costs only a few hundred dollars to look like a millionaire anywhere in the world, so anyone can do it.

9. Your individual success is not everyone's success, so don't be an imitator, be an innovator.

10. PLEASE READ EVERYTHING CAREFULLY AND NEVER RUSH INTO ANYTHING YOU DO NOT UNDERSTAND.

Tip: If you pay attention long enough you will notice the huge differentiator between successful people and everyone else, and that is *accountability*.

112

True successful people take responsibility for every known or unknown circumstance whether they are good or bad. They don't jump to conclusions and hurry up with excuses to put the blame on someone else for their mishap. They exemplify true leadership and find results quickly to fix any situation that arises.

You are responsible for your own success not your boss, not the job market, not anything you rely on. When you embrace responsibility for every outcome in your life, you start leading the life you want, and most people will follow. Suddenly you start finding that everyone around you begin to like you and respects you more, some might not, but its reality. Be an entrepreneur, a manager or an employee who acknowledges their mistakes and take the steps necessary to improve your life and move forward into growth.

"Be that person on the path to wealth that becomes the driver, rather than just be the passenger."

Key Reminders:

Build Trust - At every level of your organization, family or business insist that everyone understands the importance of keeping their word and staying committed to their values and yours. Customers, co-workers, and family members want to know that they can depend on you.

Act Decisively - Learn to make decisions promptly instead of waiting for every piece of data. Some imperfect decisions you make now can be corrected later, rather than waiting for the best answers to come when it is too late, just "move correctly" when making certain decisions if you have to be hasty.

Keep Records – Always document your activities carefully and wantonly. Good records will help to preserve ideas, establish your credibility, and prove your point when the facts aren't clear. This applies to finances, employees, goals, and everything else for which you and your organization are responsible for.

Be Optimistic – I have mention this multiple times in the book that we need to maintain a positive attitude throughout all things and without being oppressive. The future looks brightest for those who seek the lambent side of everything so make it a habit to always be inventive and hopeful instead. Even if you find yourself in the worst situations, there is always something good and positive that can come from it no matter what.

Be Patient - Concentrate on incremental progress and don't rush everything. Overnight sensations and megahit victories are usually illusions facilitated by months or years of quiet effort that nobody likes to talk about. That is why establishing a habit of slow but steady progression will build up everyone's confidence and minimize the risk of diving in stupidly.

Always Take Risk – It is different when you are safe versus when playing safe; sometimes taking bold risk to move forward can change everything you ever wanted. Even when all the other factors are totally confusing and cryptic, you should position yourself to predict potential success when possible.

As entrepreneurs and leaders, we all have personal feelings towards things we lose or gain at times. But as human beings many of us are not even prepared for the magnitude and longanimity of our emotions when things do happen in our daily lives.

You will notice how swiftly our moods change due to circumstances that don't go a particular way, making some of us doubtful in the firmness of our minds. But rest assure that these feelings are normal and appropriate when you do experience them, so we all must come to terms when dealing with these emotions in our business and our family life.

Learn to accept a loss and see it as a lesson

If you know that the relationship is a total lost, quit fighting it. You are going to lose more than just a house, a car, a lover, wife, or a husband, even thousands or millions of dollars. You will start dating new people and still lose them for various reasons, even if they asked you not to call or text anymore just let it go. It will benefit you more in the end than them.

Turn anger, jealousy, or resentment into a motivating force

Don't carry around your anger or any other negative emotion whether it has happened to you in the pass or it's happening right now. It is best to keep working through these emotions to resolve them, rather than to keep bottling them up. Many of us have siblings who stole money and didn't give it back; there are so-called friends that didn't hire us for jobs we wanted and later gave it to a stranger. Some of us got denied for credit cards, loans, and travel Visa applications, so what? WE ARE NOT ENTITLED TO ANYTHING, and rejection will always come. So, you should address and examine each matter carefully to take all the correct measures first before doing anything stupid. One of the biggest acts of relief you can give yourself, is to focus forward and not on the past, because it is already gone.

It is easier to forgive yourself, than to expect forgiveness from others

In our lifetime we have made so many mistakes, hurt so many people, even disrespected them, you name it. But when we apologize or try to make up for it, asking for forgiveness doesn't always mend the issue(s). Acknowledge that we can't fix everything and just forgive yourself and make peace with it. (Colossians 3:12-13 KJV)

Remember we can't please everybody or fix everyone's problem. And how can you save everybody from the things that are dangerous out there? You can't, not even your children.

Let the past mistakes be a bridge to better choices in the present

Remember to keep a mental list of all the stupid things you have ever done up until today, whether it was helpful or hurtful. With that take ownership of these L's (lessons) to grow and challenge yourself. Then you will improve and master these errors on your path or for someone else's. These "L" will be your guide not to make them twice or thrice again.

Turn every small opportunity that slipped once, into a triumph for the next time

So many of us had the opportunity to make millions at an early age, some pass on the chance to confess their feelings to a crush, and some miss that final moment to say goodbye to a loved one. Never hold back a simple gesture to even say "thank you" to a stranger that helped in a major way. Because when those opportunities pass, you can only wish you had done something differently. Stop wasting time on it because it doesn't help; this only takes away your awareness from the real opportunities in front of you.

I believe from all the support you can get in being a better person, your best achievements in all areas of life will mainly come from *self-help* and making that full commitment to grow yourself daily. In Jim Kwik's book called *Limitless*, he lays out some great principles and concepts of how our brain works through *God's* divine creation. Kwik explains how we can release these untapped resources and brain power we don't use. And it doesn't matter what stage we are in right now, paving our own path to the success is never impossible.

Although there are a lot of people who still spend their days on nonproductive ideas or things that usually become extremely hard for them to break away from. I believe every human is a genius in their own sphere or realm of thinking. And no one has the right to determine your fate or compare you, because of your color, background, ethnicity, or social status doesn't matter.

The same things that can contribute to your success, can also lead to your downfall.

In our everyday lives we come across people who usually present themselves as friends. Eventually we come to trust them and spend time with them for different reasons, but their true nature will always show itself. Some you meet will mistreat you or ignore you when you need help, while others will use you as a tool for their own gains. These people can be difficult to mark at times, making a devilish agenda intractable to understand and what their intentions are. But they tend to fall into some categories which I have simply narrowed down so you will know them.

1. The Fake Praiser's

Tell me who doesn't love to be complimented in one way or another? This is in our nature. But everyone should beware of these fake praises and how they come off. People who are considered fake praiser's can enrapture you with words and appreciation to get closer to you.

The big question is why do they want to get closer to you so quickly? Always ask yourself, what are their goals? Thinking out loud it could be they have confidence issues, right? They want you to teach them new things, maybe share ideas; sometimes they are genuinely kind and favorable people. But it could also mean they want something very specific from you and not your friendship. 1 John 4:1 KJV says *Beloved, believe not every spirit, but try the spirits whether they are of God: because many false prophets are gone out into the world.*

2. The Manipulators

One of the most treacherous forms of fake people or friends to have around is a manipulator. They are also difficult to catch sometimes, seeing that they're highly effective and skilled in earning your trust, when they get your friendship, their devious intentions usually come out. A righteous businessperson, friend or family member will always take into consideration your thoughts and your feelings. But the manipulator has no good reason or desire for your feelings; you are only a pawn to move in order to get what they want. So don't expect them to stick around once they have gotten everything from you.

Avoid them at all cost.

3. The Social Hypocrites

These are the acquaintances, business associates and so-called friends that ONLY see you as a product, an item or an image that only makes them look good in the public eyes. So, whether it is on T.V., social media, for press or marketing that's how you are labeled. In their minds they are constantly judging everyone who connects and socialize with you, they even go as far as to disaffiliate themselves when you fall off in your career. All they see is a means to an end to climb the social ladder. So, like the manipulators they only try to associate if it suits them.

118

4. The Copy Machine

These are the people or businesses that are fans or admirers. Unlike the fake praiser's, and social hypocrites, the copy machine is willing to lower or change aspects of their personality or character, just to imitate yours. It then becomes hard for them to be "original" and find their own identity. Hence, feeding off your image drives or fuel their ego which sometimes make their end goals uncertain. Possibly in their eyes, they see a unique facet to your personality or image that they want. But I believe real friends and good business practices comes from challenging each other, with ideas and good sportsmanship. We all can grow and find out more about each other if we take on our own identity. Everyone will remain a copy machine if they don't train their brains or use their gifts.

5. The Pretenders

These are the ones who act like a friend to you, but only when it pleases them. They can also be helpful and appear supportive at times, but there is no truth or loyalty in pretending to be someone's friend. Most of the time they're only present because they need a favor or to borrow items from you that never gets returned. We all know people like this, and rarely do the true ones stick around when you hit rock bottom or there to help you back up. The real pretenders will never show up when things get tough. So don't be fooled by them.

6. The Judas

Unlike the other categories on this list, the Judas might have been a true friend, a companion, or an associate at one point. They may have been important to you and can still be, but "secretly" much as changed and you don't know it. The Judas will act like a true friend around you, but they're always conspiring to betray you and your trust. Sadly, the Judas is only apparent after they have broken the bond or done great damage to your reputation.

7. The Rivals

These are the ones who appear to be more competitive rather than being supportive in your endeavors. All of us know someone or have people like this in our families, the workplace and who they acquaint with occasionally. For example, if you mentioned something great that you did or about a friend, they immediately shift the attention on them just to overshadow their insecurities. That's a rival. Every goal you make or an accomplishment that you have is a challenge for them, it's never something to be celebrated. If you get a new car, they get one too, if you dress for an occasion, they try to out dress you. Rivals take on everything you do; they don't try to elevate themselves, only to become better than you. What should be love and support is just jealousy and competition and when they can't out do you, they move to spoil your enjoyment by becoming a *frenemy*.

Chapter 13

Common Mistakes When Building a Business For Success

"The only real mistake is the one from which we learn nothing." —***Henry Ford***
(American industrialist)

Many businesses are created out of a passion, and while passion can be a main motivator, it does not hold great signification to start one. But planning out exactly how you're going to turn that vision into a successful business is perhaps the most valued step, between the idea and the reality. Aside from that there are only so many precautions you can take to minimize the risks in business, whether you hope to start your own, working up to the corporate ladder or just to support your employer's success the best way you can. You must first understand how to grow a business so it will survive and remain successful throughout its lifetime.

Furthermore, being an entrepreneur is a "risky" profession, but don't get discourage and turn away because you didn't think it through. That risk becomes significantly more manageable once you go and test it against a well-crafted business plan. It is necessary to draft up realistic revenues and expense projections, devising operational duties, and understanding the competitive market for that geographical area. All this can help reduce the risk factors from an unsteady way of living and how to make money.

Having a plan will allow you not to leave anything to chance, by making better decisions and lowering your blood pressure. Giving you the clearest possible view of the future for your business or your brand.

From data gathered over a period, these are some of the more common mistakes that most businesses make and end up failing:

1. **No market need:** Many businesses become over packed with product and services that many people don't want, and sometimes can be found anywhere, always research what the market demands.

2. **Inadequate team support:** It is very important you surround yourself with the right people to help you run your business and build your brand.

3. **Competition:** This is a common threat to everyone, because it can be tough to generate a steady profit when you have a lot of competitors in your niche. Always try to outperform everybody regardless.

   Study your market that you know everything about the other players and what they do in the industry. You don't want to be caught off guard by a rival's new idea that you get so defensive against what the competition is up to. Try to learn to adapt quickly.

4. **Pricing:** Some entrepreneurs will price their products or services too high or too low that it becomes so damaging to their sales goals. This is very destructive to most small businesses especially with startups.

5. **Adaptability:** Most business or services will sometimes lack the ability to adapt over time to the changes in the market. This usually involves the upturn in the demand, the people's interests, and style change. The business must now be able to change what is required to fill the customer's needs.

Not all businesses will be able to do this but try to upgrade and expand where you see it necessary.

6. **Lack of authenticity and transparency**: Businesses that lack authenticity and transparency will fail. Without the customer's needs in sight and a real focus on the right things, most businesses can easily lose the consumer's trust.

7. **Inability to control expenses**: It's easy to spend when the coffers are full. But having a fastidious sense to control the company's expenses is another practice. Much of this comes back to the founder's personal money usage; so always ensure that you master your spending habits to avoid these issues.

8. **Failure to create the proper business systems**: Selling on the internet is not the only automation required to run a successful business, think of other means that will boost long term growth. What are the business systems you need to put in place? Research and implement these systems. Think about CRM (Customer Relationship Management) systems, financial audits, company policies and work procedures that also need to be created as well.

There are more mistakes to avoid in any business but listing out everything won't allow you to grow in the areas where you are needed. I know learning from our mistakes will make us stronger, smarter, and more prepared for the future.

*No matter what you know, you cannot rush greatness — **Ralton Thompson***

Planning for the seasonal impacts on your business

The secret to getting ahead is getting started — **Mark Twain** *(American writer)*

No matter what type of business you run or function in, there are certain key elements that will influence the core decisions you make every day. And this is mainly centered on the products or services you offer. Due to the constant changes in the marketplaces and the economy, planning before the change comes will determine how you weather the storms ahead. Perhaps one of the most difficult challenges of this life or any business is to adequately "prepare for the future."

Niccolò Machiavelli the Italian philosopher who is credited as the father of political science. Counsels us that *change is inevitable*, and we need to be adaptable if we wish to experience continued success. He said, *"Whosoever desires constant success must change his conduct with the times."* So, knowing what truly lies ahead will always be challenging, even with the most thorough research and the best available information. Predictions are merely just speculations.

These are some are key factors that can impact your business:

Economic elements

There are certain economic factors that can have an influence on your business or services, these can be change in patterns, trends, or emerging "crisis." Some may include changes in legislation, government, **taxes**, business funding, a pandemic or just the overall instability of the economy. For example, if you run a clothing company, and there is a fluctuating cost of material versus labor, that may affect how much products you can manufacture at a time and how much you can actually charge the consumers for the service.

Leadership

This is where a lot of attention is required; a true leader has to fulfill the business purpose and its mission. But you must first become the "right" kind of leader for your business or your brand. Appointing the right person is important, because they will either steer the business towards ultimate success or they can be its ultimate failure. Decide who will lead, but only if you have too many hats wearing. So having a vision is expected from its leaders, that the company can grow and increase its productivity and profits. A true leader will influence how the business is run, within itself, and give value to the customers and clients. But a poor leader can negatively affect the company's performance and the mandate which is detrimental to its survival.

Marketing and Advertising

The practice of marketing has been known for over a millennia, is has grown more businesses and brands than anything else to date, but some businesses often have a notion that the growth and profit of a business, is dependent solely on the kind of business products/services they offer alone. So, if you decide to run a business-to-business (B2B) company or a business-to-client (B2C) brand or just services, this will be the main source for sales and promotion.

Marketing and advertising as evolved over the decades, and we must change with the times. These are my tips to grow your business and services no matter what is happening.

1. Awareness

Is your company the best kept secret in your industry?

There are probably millions of potential customers who would buy your products or work with your company, if they knew you actually exist. So, raising the awareness is central to marketing. But how can you raise awareness? You must first get your "business name or brand" out into the marketplace. Do it consistently and impressively in the same way, but not to everyone, just largely to your target niche.

There are hundreds of ways to raise awareness. You can advertise with a blogger, partner up with an event planner who does concerts, shows, or even weddings. You can even speak at conferences to get in front of potential buyers or clients, run online ads and campaigns to promote your business or products. Try to get on a radio show, maybe a podcast and issue a press release. Start attending industry events while you run webinars in partnership with trade associations to promote your solutions and new ideas. And those are just a handful of the ways that companies raise awareness, which impacts their ability to attract new customers and grow.

2. Lead generation

Today lead generation is regarded as the steps or process of identifying and sourcing potential customers for business products or services. This is currently ranked as a new wave for B2B and B2C marketers. Because business awareness and lead generation go together in the marketing world, you can spend a lot of money trying to generate leads yourself. But if you have no credible presence or awareness in the market, very few prospects will do business with you. So, employing the means of lead generation tactics will help you advance your growth faster.

3. Product or Service Promotion

This is an element of cross-selling or endorsement which acts separately but is also a part of your business image. Be mindful not to become complacent when promoting quality over quantity with your products or services. Because marketing does not only to highlight the existence of the business in the marketplace, but it also heightens your business ambitions.

It might seem different, but nothing has a bigger impact on your business success than the additional *value* you place on your products or services. Remember you are selling your service or your products to clients who see a need for it, and not your image alone. This can be done by tapping into their emotions or their daily lives to get their attention. Spend time researching and asking, what does the marketplace want? And decide how to address this. You're planning the future success of your business so make sure that you understand your customers' wants and needs.

Sales

1. Inadequate Time Spent Selling

Time is the most valuable commodity you can never get back, so monitor how you're spending your time. Ask yourself, "is manual data entry eating up your time?" Do you take all day to craft a single email? And are you struggling to keep your customers information in order? There are always other solutions. Not because we do things a certain way, doesn't mean there isn't a better way to do it. Never assume all actions will bring improvement.

2. Selling to the Wrong People

Are you the C.E.O, C.F.O, Marketing Director, Sales rep, and Accounting Officer all at the same time? Well, that's too many hats to be wearing all at once. In the beginning when you start out, yes, but if you have enough revenue streams, it is feasible to start assigning these positions to other people. The role of everyone is vital, that you're not targeting the wrong audience or the wrong prospects.

Your focus and direction must be in the right markets; because you will not be able to close every deal, STOP TRYING TO BE EVERYWHERE AT ONCE. Most business waste time with non-interested buyers or customers, just find the right people and devote yourself in going after those leads that will want your products or services.

3. Relying on Technology to Close Deals

Advantages and Disadvantages

Technology can influence any business anywhere, but does it affect other businesses in other industries? Yes, the business decisions you will make are based on your vision and the growth for your company. For example, if you have a manufacturing business that introduces a new type of loading machinery which packs and seals five times (5x) faster on an assembly line. It will later reduce the need for more factory workers. And the management decision you will have to make now is to lay off a percentage of your employees, right? Even though it might lead to more savings in labor cost in the long run, you will then have unemployed individuals and disgruntled ex-workers.

If you choose to automate most of your operations and increase the way you generate sales, then the use of various enablement tools and technology can now be more helpful to your business and others. But it's also important to remember that technology alone will not improve your sales performance or the occupancy in the marketplace. Instead, work with your team to brainstorm ways to cut out unnecessary and inefficient systems, which will not be productive. Only invest in each new technology or system once, after you figure out the right process that works. Then, document it and make sure your staff or team members know how to follow it.

Retention & Growth

Will customers be loyal and continue to do more business with you each year?

It is important you are ensuring the customers come back and keep buying your product or using your service. *Consistent* customer communication is mandatory, but do not be overwhelming. Use communication channels like radio ads, flyers, or social media etc. to share updates with your customers so you can remain relevant. Additionally, it is better to keep up with what's trending today, that way you can create campaign ads to up-sell and cross sell your services or your products.

Limited or No Training

Running a business will require a lot of time, management training and a balanced mental focus, but it's worth it. In fact, according to studies, most individuals who complete a highly rated management training course or mentorship program can increase their business revenue by ten times (10x) its current earnings.

You must become more resourceful and dedicated to yourself, so that training and learning becomes a part of your daily development. Better yet, communicating regularly with your team and establishing good set behaviors and processes will definitely build ethics, especially when it comes to new hires. Remember, training should be an ongoing process and not just a one-time thing. It is actively evaluating your training methods to make adjustments as you see it fit.

There is always room for improvement in everything.

Partnerships

There are different types of partnership that a business or a brand can seek out based on their preference and location. These may include mergers, acquisitions, internal partnerships between departments or external partnerships with like-minded companies that decide to join for a specific service or cause. Partnerships can be a key influence in any business giving the company valuable exposure and publicity within the corporate sphere, which might lead to broader customer base and a larger financial backing.

If you're going to start a business and have one or more partners, it might seem practical to form a business partnership, right? But this structure only allows you to have limited controlled ownership of the business or company. A lot of times forming a partnership might make sense to us, but it's not the only option we have. Before you form a partnership, there are the pros and cons of this business structure you must know.

Listed are some of the advantages of having a business partner(s).

1. You will have extra help

When you have a business partner or multiple partner(s) around you, it then becomes easier to divide up the work, they can get much more done over a shorter period and save you money. Partners might be able to take on more task rather than going at it alone and lowering the risk. So as a single business owner you will have to juggle many tasks and typically you will get surrounded by constant busyness and late nights.

2. Additional knowledge and experience

One of the major benefits a partner can bring to your business is additional skill sets that you don't have. So, you might have a lot of knowledge about the products or services, but you don't know how to run a business or how to find the right markets.

3. You have less financial burden

If you're starting a business for the first time depending on where you are, this can be expensive. But don't be discourage by the overhead expenses, or retail space that may carry a high price tag now, having a partner can ease this financial weight. So instead of paying for everything, you and your partner can split the cost. A business partner's financial contributions will allow you to afford more things up front and avoid a large sum of debt when starting out.

4. Less paperwork to start out

Starting a partnership isn't difficult. In most cases you might only have to submit some local paperwork, unlike other entities that have to file with the courts or the federal government.

However, all partners involved in any business transaction must sign a partnership agreement. Creating and signing this document is quite unambiguous than filling out the paperwork for other business structures. But do more research just to be on the safe side.

5. There are fewer tax forms

Being in a partnership can also circumvent additional business taxes, which means you don't have to fill out or file certain tax forms. Instead, here in the United States, taxes are passed through to the business owners and they share the profits and losses on your individual tax return forms. This makes each partner liable for paying any additional taxes and not only you.

Here are the disadvantages of having a business partner(s).

1. You can't make decisions on your own

When you're in a partnership, you cannot act independently or for your own desires. Due to the initial structure, you must work with your partner(s) to make certain business decisions, or at least disclose them with your partner(s).

If any partner acts alone and makes an ill-advised decision, all partner(s) are responsible for the decision and the results. Because each partner represents the company or business, they cannot be held independently responsible.

2. You will have to divide the profits

When you run a business by yourself, even with employees or independent contractors, you still have more advantages to gain all the profits from the services or products you offer.

But in a partnership, you must share the profits based on the contractual agreement or depending on how many partners you have. And this sometimes results in a small return.

3. You will have disagreements

It is a well-known fact that when people in general have to work together, it sometimes causes contention between them. At some point you and your partner(s) will mostly like have disagreements, whether they are small or great. But hopefully it will not cause harm or division. Some partners eventually get uncomfortable doing business with each other and when this happens, dissolving a partnership gets tedious. In most cases you have to redistribute profits and losses, change your business structure, and then start to assign new responsibilities among the remaining partners, if any. With luck, you had prepared a "partnership exit strategy" to elude the situation.

One of the most controversial disagreements in business history was between the two Dassler brothers. Adolf "Adi" the one who designed the shoes and his brother Rudolf "Rudi" who was the salesman for the company. Eventually, their disagreements on the direction of the company led them to part ways and split the company down to the last cent. Rudi moved on to create the **Puma** brand while Adi continued and created **Adidas**. This historic feud gave birth to the world's most two iconic brands up until today. But what really caused the disagreement between the brothers' and why they decided not to reconcile? After years it is still speculation in the media. But for those reasons whether personal or unprofessional; please ensure your partnerships are based on *trust* and *integrity*.

4. You are not separate from the business

This part of the business is not talked about a lot, but a partnership is not a separate legal entity from you and the other partners. So, in any matter concerning the business, all partners are legally and financially responsible. Also take into consideration that if the business faces legal problems, you won't be considered separate from the business.

Even if the business is unable to repay any debts, loss or even becomes bankrupt. Debt collectors, banks or Government agencies can come after your personal money or assets.

5. You're taxed individually

When your partnership is established through the proper channels, being taxed individually can be an advantage, but it's also a disadvantage. Generally, business taxes have lower fees than individual taxes. Because the taxes are passed through the business to you and your partner(s), you might collectively pay more than if you paid business taxes.

Chapter 14

Learning the Laws of the Land and Self-Governance

"No man is above the law and no man is below it: nor do we ask any man's permission when we ask him to obey it" — **Theodore Roosevelt** *(26th U.S. President)*

In the United States and other countries in the world, it seems they have laws and regulations to govern just about everything right? But most people don't like rules and regulation since they usually mean someone is telling us what to do or keep us from doing what we want to do. We try to avoid these laws and not obey them, yet to live in a civilize society, we MUST have rules and regulation to follow and maintain order.

You may be wondering why I am talking about laws in this book. Well to be successful at keeping your wealth or any possessions in this world, you must also know and understand the laws that govern your land. It gives you a stronger advantage to put in place measures to secure your wealth and your safety. So, who gets to make these rules? Where do they come from? And what happens when we break them? These are the questions this book will seek to answer for you.

Understanding the Importance of the Laws on the Land

To see the importance of anything you must first understand its nature. Laws are systems of rules which a community or a country uphold as measures to demand its citizens to comply, but if not followed certain penalties are enforced. Laws are in place to protect our general safety and ensure our rights as citizens against aggressive abuse by other people, organizations, or even by the government itself. These laws exist at the local, state, and national levels:

If you work for any organization or business right now, it is important to understand their work policies, rules and the laws that govern their institution. There are more state and local level laws, for small businesses and corporations in their guidelines, so pay attention to those "if" you're going into business for yourself or "if" you're already in business.

To give an example, the United States Department of Agriculture and other federal agencies will setup inspection laws and guidelines for food productions, so that the commodities which show up in our supermarkets are safe for consumption or usage. That's one reason to be aware of the laws they impose on manufacturers and distributors for you to live a better and more functional life.

Another aspect of using the law is to ensure you visit proper health care facilities. All doctors and nurses are required to be licensed and trained individuals, readily available to tend to your very needs. If anything should go wrong these same institutions must be held accountable for any "unlawful mishandling" or cause of death. Someone in authority must have *ascendancy* for governing our livelihood, whether it is us or a regulatory body.

We must be well-informed of the laws that protect our rights as citizens, which includes but not limited to our basic rights of freedom such as freedom of speech, religion, and duty. But laws that also protect us against discrimination due to our race, age, gender, or disabilities.

John Locke one of the most influential political philosophers of the modern era, described in the *Two Treatises of Government* that all men and women are by nature free and equal against claims that God had made all people to naturally subject to a monarch. He argued that people have rights, such as the right to life, liberty, and property that has a foundation, which is independent of the laws of any society.

Locke made arguments saying that since governments truly exist by the consent of the people, in turn they should be obligated to them, and to protect the rights of the people and promote the public good. But governments tend to fail as they promised to do for the people and so can be resisted and replaced with new governments.

All these arguments being stated can be true, but as citizens and residents you must realize that waiting around for our governments to change things won't always be in our best interest. So, focus on the goals and the purpose you are pursing right now, with "hopes" that any governing party in power will enact laws and policies that will eventually benefit your growth or progress and not just them alone.

Understanding the laws of Self-Governance

These are laws that will help you govern your success and explain in-depth function as humans. Many of us have a rebellious spirit when we hear about laws, even to our own benefit, we either deny it or ignore it. No one wants to hear that I need to have laws that govern my everyday actions and thoughts, but in truth and in fact we do. *In order to know what's good we must also know what's bad.*

Self-governance or self-rule is the ability to practice all the necessary functions of control without the interference from an external authority. It is closely related to various philosophical and socio-political concepts such as autonomy, independence, self-control, self-discipline, and sovereignty. It may also refer to the internal conduct of an organization such as social groups, affinity groups, legal bodies, families, religions, and political establishments of various levels.

In ancient Greek philosophy, Plato proposed the concept of self-mastery as the ability to be one's own master; he states that individuals or groups cannot achieve freedom unless they govern their own pleasures and desires, and instead they will be in a state of enslavement.

137

Conclusively what Plato was saying is that this principle is not only a fundamental moral freedom, but also as a necessary condition not to be enslaved by political influence or any political structure.

John Locke furthers this principle to say that genuine freedom requires cognitive self-discipline and self-governance. Given that all humans' have the capacity to do this, it is then the source of all freedom in this area. Learn this and keep this in your thoughts, *"freedom is not a possession, but it is an activity."*

Methods of self-governance

Self-governance is usually comprised of the following:

Code of conduct — this outlines acceptable behavior within oneself, a unit, or a group. It can include a legal or ethical code (e.g., Mission Statement, Values or Employees Break policy in a workplace or business).

Exclusion — it is a way of ensuring external authority or influence does not become involved unless a certain standard is satisfied.

Purpose — this objective will promote your intended function or goals.

Discipline — when you practice disciplinary procedures within yourself, you obey the laws and rules that is set up and you live by them.

Control — the ability to suppress or restrict habits, tendencies and outside influences from your environment or unit.

Solutions — a means of registering and resolving problems or disagreements with friends, family members, unions, or business associates, and give closure if needed.

Natural Law and Natural Rights

What Is Natural Law?

Natural Law can be defined as an ingrained entity of moral principles which is the foundation of humans having the intrinsic values that typically governs our reasoning and behavior. Natural law maintains the basis that these rules of right and wrong is deeply rooted in people and is not *created* by our society or any judicial system we live in.

So, without forcing anyone, I believe these laws are the ones we should never change because they existed long before us. There is a certain authenticity that is applied to all people, regardless of the place they lived or the agreements they make. For that reason, there is a distinction that is created between natural law and positive law which I will explain more.

Understanding Natural Law

To understand what Natural law does, we must consider it is also the universal moral standard that is innate in all humans and these standards should not be form based on just societal influences. Human beings are NOT taught natural law, but instead we "discover it" by constantly making choices for good instead of evil. In some scenarios other individuals are influenced against their better judgement, while some schools of thought believe that natural law is passed to humans by a way of divine presence. Although natural law mainly applies to the area of ethics and philosophy, it is also widely used in theoretical economics, and that is something you can do research on.

Positive Law vs. Natural Law

How does Positive Law work?

There is a divergence to what is known as "positive law" or "man-made law," compared to the theory of natural law. It is believed that our civil laws should be based on morality, ethics, and what is fundamentality correct. This is defined by rules and common law practices and may or may not be considered natural laws.

Examples of positive law can include speed limits that are set for individuals to drive on the roads, the age of consent that anyone can legally purchase alcohol or the number of hours anyone should work for a company. What a lot of people might not perceive is when authorities are preparing positive laws, these governing entities base them on the recognition of natural law, so one law can't work without the other.

Romans 13:1-3 of the KJV bible says, [1] Let every soul be subject unto the higher powers. For there is no power but of God: the powers that be are ordained of God. [2] Whosoever therefore resisteth the power, resisteth the ordinance of God: and they that resist shall receive to themselves damnation. [3] For rulers are not a terror to good works, but to the evil. Wilt thou then not be afraid of the power? do that which is good, and thou shalt have praise of the same.

Natural law is also separate from another law called *divine law*. It was originally mentioned with the **Laws of God** revealed to us through the prophets and other inspired writers in the Christian tradition. So Divine law can only be experienced through **God's** special revelation and to those individuals whom it was revealed. In the holy scriptures *God* specifically indicates who are bounded by this law. And while Natural law can be discovered by rationale and applies to all people, Divine Law is not the same.

KEY TAKEAWAYS

The theory of natural law suggests that humans possess an intrinsic sense of right and wrong that governs our reasoning and behavior.

Natural law is constant throughout time and across the earth because it is based on human nature, and not on culture or customs.

Foundation Laws

Foundation Laws are subject to different meanings and in different areas, but it refers to the introductory grounds or principles necessary to establish and build a structure or framework for anything. For example, it can be a building, a relationship, a company or even life itself. On that note, it also the same principle from which I wrote this book and the process I underwent to convey my message to you. These are the same ethics necessary to conduct any business and to keep its survival and longevity. I believe foundational laws should be kept for records and be well documented to prepare others on what is expected and what is required to build a long-lasting structure.

Foundation laws are the preliminary proof required to admit evidence that works. But to challenge the foundation of any structure or relationship, you must first test the grounds of what is presented to qualify the evidence used as the truth. For example, do Millionaires really make more money from reading books? Can eating healthy help me live longer? And if I invest my money wisely, will it grow or not? This should be a well-focused challenge that is necessary to allow you to conclude and evaluate the standard of the foundation evidence being suggested. Because it then allows the challenger a reasonable opportunity to correct any inadequacy or absence from the foundation.

KEY TAKEAWAYS

Foundation laws are essential to everything we build and create.

Foundation laws should be kept for records to prove its accuracy and qualify the evidence used in its arguments for its basis.

Creation Laws

This law is contrary to scientific laws, but if you believe in the Holy bible, it offers us nothing conflicting to what is written in the Scriptures. For generations there have been speculations and theories to give scientific grounds to explain something, such as the origin of the universe, or life itself. My purpose of introducing this law is to open our minds not to take everything we are taught in schools, from certain books and what others try to impose on your belief system. There will be many that don't see the relevance of this law, while others will accept the truth of the Holy bible. I just want people to understand that scientific laws are generally expressions of principles that have been established based on facts or research, and not all are evidence are true to their claims.

While innovative ideas and "creative" work comes from the mind to increase economic success and build nations. I found it interesting to share it with my readers and you might be asking why? I believe it will add more value to a lot of people's life experiences, as they go out in the world every day to "create" new beginnings. And not just from the societal teachings but from the natural existence of these laws that governs our *creativity* without human boundaries. Keep in mind that these laws also allow us to experience reality and not the ones society writes about and dictates.

Chapter 15

Paving your Path to Success

Success usually comes more easily to someone who already had it...because they know the path!

Many of us try to find this materialized success by following some easy or simple path, while some try to pave a new road not traveled yet. But when we are clearing and laying out any path to success it is anything but easy, believe me! Marcus Garvey once said *"You can only make the best out of life by knowing and understanding it. To know, you must fall back on intelligence of others who came before you and have left their records behind."* Garvey was a charismatic Black leader who organized the first important American Black nationalist movement and later broke the barriers that previously prevented colored people from entering certain sectors and business organizations.

Before writing this book, I had countless opportunities and paths I could have taken, but I wanted to try a new course. Today I am continuously learning and growing because of my choices. While it is not easy, I have found some specific precepts that will help you remain focused and can lead you on a path of personal success from my experience:

First you need to be **UNGUARDED,** but only temporarily. Start by opening up to the right people and not just anyone, because around them you can share the things you are struggling with and seek advice on how to improve yourself. There are still good people out there who want to help. More importantly, surround yourself with those who will support your dreams and vision; these are the same people on their own journey who will understand you. They will see your struggles and objectives and they can be a reminder that you are doing an amazing job.

Secondly be **OPEN-MINDED**. Leave behind any expectations associated with what was in the past and focus on what will be. You might have held titles as an Executive Director, a manager, or a top performer in a corporate firm. Think of what will define your success today in this new age that's beginning. What I can tell you is that it's not what society as placed in our feeble minds, your success will likely be different when you find out for yourself.

Your experience and possessions can sometimes imprison your progress, but do not let that imprison your dreams. Despite what you might know, you will only need to bring a small amount of your old life with you to achieve any change.

Thirdly be **PURPOSEFUL**. Whatever you set out to accomplish, ensure you complete it. Your day is not only filled with the things you want to do. There are a lot of things you "should" do as well. Our minds can be obsessed about what we want to do, but they never get done. So be responsible in "making the time" to write down or make reminders in your phone, tablets, calendar, or sticky pads of what you plan to focus on for the day, or month and get it done. I'm never free with my work schedule, but I do make time for everything, so I never waste it.

Be **UNREFINED**, this is like allowing yourself to mess up, by making mistakes, taking calculated risk and be uncomfortable for a moment. At least this will help you to move ahead faster. Don't wait or allow lack of confidence to hold you back. Learn how to push through flaws and what needs adjustment; believe me you will quickly find success on the path you are trying to make. Remember; ***practice makes progress, not perfect.***

And lastly be **GRATEFUL.** Look back on each week, celebrate your wins, and acknowledge how far you have come in your journey. Hold yourself accountable to that main goal and to your vision for success, but don't beat yourself up to get there. There will be good days and bad days ahead, so be kind to yourself.

In my early years I've learned that whenever a person asks, what do you do for a living? They are trying to calculate the level of respect and attention they should give you. And that's why I preferred to stay low-key and be evasive in some situations. Through this experience I realize that most people do this, and it's just human nature. I usually don't dictate how people should judge or look at each other, but I do believe everyone, and everything should be respected. Because your path can turn for the worse on this journey through life, it is wise to show respect and be humble. Many of us are sometimes embarrassed about the social status or our current lifestyle because society as demonized people in certain working class. But everyone will not be successful, and everyone will not be rich. The next time you have an opportunity to recount your own story, do it. Capture your learnings from each unique moment and sometimes it only takes the right support to turn your own experiences into strategies that can pave your own path to success.

Choose a path that will represent your intentions, actions and purpose

I can remember my high school years when I use to be nervous when I made a T.V. appearance, and I was not a shy person around people or even to speak up. In the early 2000's when the internet wasn't as prominent as it is today, my old high school in Jamaica, Clarendon College High was apart a National Quiz competition that played other high schools throughout the island.

I was really good in the subject areas they assigned me, because I use to read hundreds of unusual books on general knowledge, history and everything else that normal high school kids DID NOT READ. This gave me an *uncompetitive advantage* in being apart the Quiz team back then and for those reasons I stood out.

In 2003, our team did so well in the competition that we got sponsorship from the old past student association, with traveling incentives and community support for all that hard work. Unfortunately, we only made it to the semi-finals that year and loss the match. And it wasn't that the other team was better than us, but they remain calm and was more collective, to out play us in the end. Those live T.V. appearances and other platforms made us more popular in high school and throughout the island, even in international territories from the exposure. But today its way easier for a lot of people to be marketed, promoted, and to also build their internet presence. Just chose the best platform that will show off your talents, gifts, or skills to excel your potential and purpose.

Create focus and strategies to help you move forward faster

Our brain generates roughly over 7,000 thoughts per day, and it can be more overwhelming with other activities that we perform daily. Even when we shuffle a great amount of information, there is still a limit. Because at some point we all reach a "critical mass." It starts when you miss place things, avoiding people, getting angry, struggling at work, in the home or in relationships you name it.

The problem is we need to have a balance of everything to find that source of peace, because stress will kill growth and mental focus. My methods might be common and non-traditional to a lot of people, but it works for me, so I strongly suggest everyone find and design what works best for them.

These credos have become way of life to tackle anything in my path towards success. I also use one hour (1hr) every day to improve myself, whether by reading or listening a podcast.

Get through things one day at a time

Worrying does not take away tomorrow's troubles, it takes away today's peace. Each day has enough trouble of its own." So, when life is becoming stressful, it really helps to just focus on getting through each day. I use the mornings to get centered and be ready to face the day because everything will come at you as soon you wake up. Life can feel so much easier when you face it one day at a time, but never get too comfortable.

Meditate or pray

I spend each morning praying and meditating no matter what is happening in the world, this has become law and credence in my home, so nothing disturbs this mantra. I made so much progress in my spiritual life, that my mental focus is so unplugged from all the craziness in the world. Sometimes we need to relax and take moments to reflect on the good we have, instead of complaining and get resentful of the unpleasantness that most of us face each day. I am believer in *God's* Holy teachings and His way of life for us. So, I encourage you to meditate on a calming scripture or verse from the Holy Bible (in my case) it creates a sense of peace and even lowers stress to last throughout the day, most times longer if you allow it.

Take mental breaks

It is important not to hold on to this go-go mentality because it will wear you down. We should take breaks whenever our body or our mind starts to feel burdened. Go for a walk, do some stretches, just rest your brain.

Go somewhere peaceful, I do this every day and it always feels relaxing. We all need breaks. So don't keep telling yourself that you're better off working right through, this will kill you.

Make yourself eat, no matter how crazy things are.

If you are skipping meals or even a snack it can lead to fatigue, low blood sugar, and brain fog which restricts your ability to cope. I understand we all have stresses that come in our lives constantly, but you must discipline yourself to get some real food in your body as soon as you start each day. When you eat properly you tend to feel much calmer, clear minded and more focused.

Don't ignore your body's cues for needing food and water, no matter how busy you are.

Stop making excuses

I have learned that making excuses doesn't change anything; you only avoid a problem or delay the inevitable from happening. Time will still pass regardless of what you say or do, for we know it waits for no one. Every so often we all try to do everything in our relationships, our homes, and in our businesses, but there will always be problems and things we cannot control around us. Don't always blame yourself or anyone when things don't work out according to plan.

Give yourself a Sabbath day every week (preferably Saturdays)

We live in a world that is run 24-7 and it is very easy to treat each day as an opportunity to make money or to chase some dream. For several years, I've managed to break myself into keeping the Commandments of *God* and taking Saturdays off as a *Law,* no matter how busy I am.

Whenever I'm tempted to work on a project or do some transaction, I remind myself how far I've come doing this, and I refrain from going into the worldly activities until the day as ended.

For one day out the week try to avoid doing anything that feels like work. Turn off your phone sometimes. Don't go online every minute. Take a nap. Read a great book even the Holy Bible. Spend time with your family and friends. Go for a walk with a loved one. That one day should be a day of rest, to rejuvenate and refresh your mind and give your body the energy it needs to face the trenches of life for another week. You will still get a lot done on other days, so one day won't kill you.

What if I want it all? The success, influence, and power?

I can assure you having it all is a misleading and an overly ambiguous ambition, called GREED. That being said, it is economically and psychologically impossible to have it all, no matter what anyone says on T.V. or over the internet. The Great King Solomon was once renowned as the wisest and richest man in his time. Even he could not have it all. So, it's impossible to have all of the good and none of the bad.

For instance, if you literally had all the wealth in the world, you would have to be at war with everyone else to protect it, think about it? It would make your success a short-lived one and a heavy burden to bear, plus many people have tried it and died along the way.

In the same manner it would be you wanting all the happiness in the world and none of the sorrow or pain that comes with it. You couldn't even relate to anyone with compassion, understanding or even empathy around you. This would make you unhappy at some point, but on the other hand this might be different for some people as well. Because they would have everything materially in the world yet lose their "soul" in the process. *(Mark 8 v.36-37 KJV).*

Based on this *precursory* notion, those who claim to have it all are lying. They are just conceitedly hiding the fact that they don't. Life is simply about making choices and when you choose one option, you are still saying no to many more. You can have most of what you want in life, yes, but you cannot have it all. If you really have it all, I simply believe you had both victory and defeat; celebration and disappointment; abundance and lack; with love and heartbreak, and so forth. All these experiences could have given you lessens from life. But it is totally a different notion from thinking "I want to have it all."

While on this new journey to become a more productive, there will be a cost to the get there and you must stick to those changes when you make them. Most of us are ambitious by nature, but our ambition also gives us purpose and a sense of direction in life. However, this comes at a great cost. As L.M. Montgomery said, *"We pay a price for everything we get or take in this world; and although ambitions are well worth having, they are not to be cheaply won."*

Here are some of the commonly known sacrifices that will not come cheaply.

#1. **Late nights, early mornings**

Most of your days will lead to late nights and a lot of early mornings. Occasionally you will miss a few meals, forget breaks, but importantly stay away from the late-night outings and many other unproductive events. Just stick to the success plan and get the job done. Seal it in your head that you run your day and your day doesn't run you.

Spend any extra time you have working on yourself, meeting new people, or volunteering in profitable things, these play a huge part in your success. The first cost of ambition is **time**. If you want to achieve great things, you must put in the time required.

#2. **Lots of associates, but few friends**

Unfortunately, there will be times you will have to disassociate yourself to be alone and avoid the people that don't believe in you. It is a part of the journey in achieving your goals. Use all that to fuel yourself and keep pushing forward.

*"It can be lonely at the top. But the journey to the top can be quite lonely to get there." — **Ralton Thompson***

Throughout your journey you will meet contrasting people, those who have good influences and others who have bad influences. But you will also meet the liked minded people; and those who will help you to become better in life. Staying around those people will keep you motivated, proactive and fixated on achieving your goals.

Second cost of success is **friendship**. People either inspire you or drain you, so pick them wisely.

#3. **You will be single unless...**

Your journey will most often require you to do a lot by yourself, even if you're in a relationship or not. As individuals paving our own path, sometimes others can't grasp what we are working towards. But you must ensure that you have someone who can be there a 100% for you, someone who understands and is willing to go through the same storms and struggles with you.

If this is difficult right now and you cannot find anyone, then you will be single unfortunately. *The more successful you become, the higher your standards and demands will be to find that person to match you.*

Achieving your success to others can seem monotonous, so make sure you choose the right partner. And be with someone that will uplift you and not someone that will create more problems.

Third cost of success is **love**. Choose wisely, and don't act desperate to find just anybody.

#4. **You will be misunderstood**

It's natural for people to always judge everything they don't understand, and so will it be when you start a new path to success. You must be prepared to get misunderstood because people will assume and make remarks based on their experience, their education or social upbringing. The moment you start doing something new or acting out the norm, critics will be waiting for you. And there will be at least two kinds of critics.

The first one will be the "advisable critics" who sincerely misunderstands what you're doing or just honestly have a different opinion on what you should do. The second will be the "pessimistic critics" these are the ones who are NOT interested in liking or supporting anything you do. But you have to be resilient in your choices and pay close attention to both critics.

Eventually if you know and believe in what you are doing, then listening to their opinions is good enough, but stay focus on achieving your goals and stay on "your" path, and not theirs.

The fourth cost of success is the willingness to be **misunderstood.**

#5. **People will want you to do good, but never better than them.**

The sad truth is that most people you know and the ones you don't know are not going to want you to be better than them at anything. Only a "few" who believe in your dreams and your aspirations will want more for you.

Some things will not always be clear to you or to them, but a lot of people will want your success and envy you when you get to that plateau of high achievement. Their basic instinct and thoughts are to want your work or plans to fall apart. Some people are petrified that your success somehow equates to their loss and would want you to be down at their level.

Plus, our society usually hates it when someone doesn't s conform to their ideals. But the people at the top don't conform. You will have that rare group of individuals who will be cheering for you, believing in you, and celebrating your victories with you, those are the people you will have as your support.

Fifth cost of success is the **mentality** to be tolerable of others.

"Success is not something you pursue; it is the value and growth you place on yourself" — ***Ralton Thompson***

Chapter 16

Understanding Failure: The Importance and Value from Failing

"If you are afraid of failure you don't deserve to be successful!"
   — ***Charles Barkley*** *(Former professional basketball player).*

Why is failure so important?

I have failed more times than I would like to admit, and these are not small failures; I'm talking about failures that crush my finances, complicated my relationships, and affected my mental wellness. As much as failure hurts, it is important and necessary to go through it believe it or not.

I can tell anyone reading this book has failed several times before, whether it's in a relationship you wanted to work, at a job you thought you would be great at or even trying to have children for the first time. Don't get me wrong, I don't particularly enjoy failing for any reason, but it happens, and I know failure brings life-altering lessons that can make us strong people, but ONLY if we decide.

Amongst a number of things, failure is a great teacher; its very nature can sometimes strip away your ego, your pride and any classism some people possess. Failure can mold and shape any of us through a divine intention or pursuit for happiness if that's the end goal. So, without failure, we'd be less capable of compassion, new understanding, and empathy. Failures will surprisingly help us to reach to a zenith of creativity or invention, so it's an unavoidable outcome.

Why is it so important to fail at some things before we can succeed?

When we think about failure, we usually think it's anything in a negative light right? We say that failure is hurtful, and it causes emotional turmoil and upset. And this leads to guilt and regrets in our thoughts and our function. But for those that know true failure and have bounced back, they understand that it's necessary for success.

Booker T. Washington a renowned orator and educator, advised several U.S. presidents. And he said, *"Success is to be measured not so much by the position that one has reached in life as by the obstacles which he has overcome."* Being an influential leader in the early 20th century for the African American community, he understood what was necessary to be successful.

The most successful individuals in life have failed more times than the average person. So, if you try to go through life without failing at anything, then you're not really living a life at all. Taking risks and falling flat is a part of the process; it makes us into who we should be, and not who we are.

It's through failure that we learn some of the greatest lessons life can teach us.

If you study all the famous people who have failed, it will help you to look at their failures from their perspective. I bet all of us can relate to that frustrating feeling when something did not go right on the first try. Then multiply that frustration 5,126 times. Because that's the number of trials Sir James Dyson failed with his sample prototypes over a 15 plus year period, before coming close to creating the best-selling bag-less vacuum cleaner he named after himself Dyson. This "failure and success" experience led his business to be worth billions of dollars today. And what most people don't realize is the different challenges all successful entrepreneurs have to truly go through to get where they are in life.

Like a baby learning to walk, they will fall many times until they get it. Failing might sound exigent to endure, but it's an arcane experience that is worthwhile in the end. The problem with those who control our societal depiction, is they tend to celebrate the successes of others rather than highlighting the epic journeys towards the success that is filled with trials, tribulations, and setbacks. I don't believe that this is intriguing or colorful to talk about alone.

Michael Jordan said *"I've missed more than 9,000 shots in my career. I've lost almost 300 games. 26 times, I've been trusted to take the game winning shot and missed. I've failed over and over and over again in my life. And that is why I succeed."*

Is failing necessary?

Yes, because failure is constant and unpreventable, and it is a steppingstone in your progress. There are five (5) powerful life lessons that failure will teach and instill in us. So, If you or anyone is going through a difficult time right now and as failed at anything in a major way, keep these important lessons in mind.

Lesson #1

To gain **experience**.

When we go through a test and can walk away with firsthand experience, it helps us to develop a deeper understanding of the situation we had encountered. Failing at anything is truly invaluable no matter what was lost through the experience. Because this completely alters our frame-of-mind through pain or suffering that makes us reflect on the real importance of our lives. Potentially its purpose was to transform us and improve our future self.

Lesson #2

Failure brings direct **knowledge**. This knowledge can now be utilized for future references to overcome those same failures that was inflicting the trauma in the first place. When Thomas Edison famously failed nearly 10,000 times to create a viable electric light bulb, it was from each fail attempt that he gained the knowledge to another avenue that didn't work. There was a black inventor and engineer name *Lewis Latimer*, that help play a vital role in the light bulb creation. If each time you fail, then seek help or gain more understanding so you don't repeat the same process. That same accumulated knowledge helped Edison to later on develop his ultimate success.

Lesson #3

Failing helps you to build **resilience**. If you keep failing more times than you can count and decide not to give up, then the more resilient you will become.

To achieve high success, resilience plays a great part. And while optimism is a prime component of your growth, we won't always succeed on the first try of "everything." The habit of resilience can produce a more distinguished result if you set up a game plan to win. Gone are the expectations that everything will happen overnight and right away. Because when the stones hit the fan, the true actuality of success comes with enormous work and effort to maintain.

Lesson #4

When we fail, we learn from **growing** and **maturing** quickly. We can reach a deeper understanding about our lives and why we're doing the things we do. This helps us to reflect or put things into perspective so we can grow from that situation or loss. Life was designed for us to improve on every day, so without growth we can't improve on anything.

Lesson #5

One of the biggest lessons we can learn from life's failures is **value**. It is a commodity which helps create and spread an exceeding amount of usefulness. In fact, value lies at the heart of success, but the lack of value is also a structural pillar to failure. If you list out your past failures, look on how much value you brought to the table? Could you have offered more value? And could you have prevented those failures? When you have learned to create immense value, and do it consistently, you will eventually succeed at everything you decide that is worth accomplishing.

The T.V host Oprah Winfrey is a billionaire today and has an extensive production list in her catalogue. Although she's known for giving away lavish gifts or helping many people, her failures helped built her career as well. Oprah was fired from her first TV job as an anchor in Baltimore, Maryland. And in 2013, she reflected on these experiences during a Harvard commencement speech and said, *"There is no such thing as failure. Failure is just life trying to move us in another direction."*

When we're going through our failures, it's hard to recognize the importance of it. It's like going down a one-way street without no lights and you have no clarity to see what you're going to hit, that is scary, but we must learn from it. A better understanding does come from failing after, hence why it's unavoidable, even if you have everything in place.

You might ask, how do I recover from failure? Well here are some ways you can do this.

Ignore all the disbelievers

When you fail, surely there will be the people saying, "I told you so," and "You should have listened to me." Disregard those people and keep your failures to yourself sometimes, you don't need any judgmental comments from others who can't help or support you.

It's okay if you fail. But it's not okay to give up

Even if you failed and it was extremely painful, it's NOT okay to just give up easily. Keep moving forward until you succeed. Success will reward you more when you reach it.

In the summer of 2009, I started my first small business at age 23 in Jamaica; it was a cellphone store in Cave Valley, St Ann. And I'll be honest I had no idea of the risk I was getting in, but I wanted to learn and see what progress I would make. At that time the first step was even harder just to get the authorize retailer contract from the phone company. But with *God's* help a family business owner got us the contract within months. Long story short, I sold a few phones over a period, but we didn't make a lot of sales, plus weeks would pass by and we had no money to cover certain store expenses along with other community issues, so I had to close the business.

"Winning isn't everything but wanting to win is."
— *Vince Lombardi (America football coach*

Revisit your goals that you don't fail often

Did you have a clear or a set goal in the past? And were these goals realistic? Start by revisiting any past errors you made, to see if those goals were clear to begin with. Sometimes our failures come from not setting the right goals in the right way. Not only that, we must also track and analyze them on a monthly, weekly, and daily basis, because it saves time.

Failure is never the end of the road for anyone; I know as long as you don't give up on yourself, you can still achieve the impossible and push past the old limitations. If you still believe in your goals, you have not failed.

Create a strategic action plan

If you want to recover from failure quickly, then always have an **Action Plan**. First, see that your goals are laid out as planned and setup how you're going to achieve them as well. Whenever we have an action plan, you can design a methodical way of achieving these goals faster. But if you come to the realization that it won't be simple, then I personally suggest approach them with a more assiduous mindset and be patient.

Use failure as leverage

If you have failed many times, use it as an advantage not only to recover, but to also guide yourself in the future. Failure has always been a great platform for growth and a *nonpareil* advantage in areas that others can't see. But to leverage failure from your experiences, you must elucidate them in your mind, so they can make sense. Write them down if you need to and look on what you could have done differently every time.

Understand that it's normal to fail

Not everybody gets it right the first time. If you were to read on how many successful athletes, actors, businesses, and other individuals who failed miserably in their lives, that list of people would be so long their stories of mistakes would take up a whole day.

Always "push forward" no matter how things may turn out, you can look back on your mistakes, but it's never to give up. There are always a ton of opportunities lined up waiting for you to run to. And it is simply one of the best ways I've used to recover from failures. Remember, it's not real failure unless you throw in the towel and give up entirely. I know failure symbolize pain or disappointment and everybody try very hard to avoid it. But in the end, we should realize it's far easier to reach that understanding through the struggles than to make up one.

What will you do in the midst of failure the next time?

Again, an action plan is what helps to push past these stumbling blocks before they come. I normally make a list of every possible scenario that could play out and then have the recovery measures in case any setbacks or loss occurs. I mentioned before that revisiting your goals and adjusting them is necessary. This way you can spend more time exploring your options, but don't over think it, you're not going to jail, it's not that serious.

Failure will take you to places you don't want to go, but in the end, this will be the determining factor that molds and shape you into a stronger person. Recovering from failure naturally becomes more effortless because of the knowledge and experience you have gathered. But without *God*, going through life without failure is impossible.

Remember this quote, "an arrow can only be shot by pulling it backwards." So, when life challenges are holding you back, it just means it's going to launch you into something great when that time comes. Keep focus and keep aiming towards your goals, and never give up on anything good you believe in. American actor Bill Cosby said, *"In order to succeed, your desire for success should be greater than your fear of failure."*

DISCLAIMER:

The information provided in this section is general in nature but will not be found in common sources. It is advisable to consult with a qualified investment professional in your jurisdiction or region, for any legal and planning opinions suiting your specific situation. This specific chapter was written for educational purposes only, so if you decide to use it as a guide, you have agreed to the all the risk which follows in any event or thereafter.

"A wise investment in the right areas will pay the best interest."

— Ralton Thompson

Chapter 17

Investing for the Future

"There are three things you can do with your life: You can waste it, you can spend it, or you can invest it. The best use of your life is to invest it in something that will last longer than your time on Earth." — **Rick Warren** *(Author, Christian pastor)*

If you study modern history at least every eight to ten years, the western world particularly goes through a phase of wealth reconstruction and only a few will make it through. The people in power never tell you how bad the economy is until it's totally late. So, how can I achieve my investment goals today should be your big question? Well, if you are not saving to invest in these harsh times, then you will unfortunately be left behind. An inheritance is the greatest gift you can give to your children or grandchildren children to inherit. So, this era of decadence and economic decline is inevitable, and only savvy business ventures, or creative investments will survive it.

I have given a few money habits in the previous chapters to help guide you towards an investment fortune, so any decision you make that's not in alignment with good money practices, will determine how long you take and what route you chose to increase your earnings. For most people, a primary goal of investing is to achieve economic independence: where we all have the ability to work or not to work. For others it is to do what is pleasing and not to worry about money. But for now, the pertinent question is: how far along are you towards achieving your goals?

Do you recall the financial crisis that crashed the American economy and other parts of the world in 2008? How could anyone forget that, and it has still impacted the world up until today. For many who don't know, it was the collapse of Lehman Brothers filing the largest bankruptcy in U.S. history that signal the event and the effects of the recession that followed. It was so bad it affected everyone's income from the poor to the wealthy.

This was one of the most abject financial downturns in our generation, with huge consequences for all countries and its trading partners throughout the world. Since the Great Depression of 1929 it was regarded as the worst economic disaster. And despite the efforts of the Federal Reserve and the U.S. Department of the Treasury, the housing prices still dropped more significantly than it did in the Great Depression. Even years after the recession ended, unemployment was still above 9% excluding those who got discouraged and had basically given up looking for a job. All this was from greed in the banking world.

Fast forward to 2020, twelve years later, the coronavirus pandemic emerged mysteriously out of China and spread to all corners of the world, affecting all types of businesses and people's livelihood down to the core. Some people have experienced temporary and permanent displacement, but the closure of many businesses is on rapid slide, and some might never recover in times to come. Every social activity has slowed down not to mention the number of deaths worldwide.

So, the consequences of the pandemic are even worse for the world economy than the ones following the Global Financial Crisis in 2008. The reason I am mentioning these events, is to show that crisis, recessions, pandemics are all recurring setbacks that must come, and they will continue to happen, it's in human nature to create chaos.

So, you must plan and prepare for every possible economic situation. An *investing* is the best plan forward and through these events.

Estimate how much you'll need to invest

First, know the stability of your income and how much you can survive with each year, if or when you stop getting a paycheck. And whatever that number is (between US$10,000? -US$100,000? Or more) multiply it by 30 (or average amount of time left to retire) plus 35% will be the amount, at a "minimum" to have in your portfolio or savings when you retire. And that is excluding Government assistance, and retirement funds from other agencies.

How did I get this formula? well I gave myself an average time I want to continue working, plus adding to the rising cost of living in the U.S each year with inflation, which is an estimate or an average of 3% (Or even higher 7-10% preferably).

Now to acquire any additional money towards your retirement goals, I am neither an investment expert nor an advisor to tell you where to invest, but I will tell you what I did. I pre-calculated the amount of money at a minimum I could invest and committed to it. I then researched each investment vehicle and entity that I wanted to invest in. I had bought land in areas where I could afford it so it when it increased, I can resell it for more, and now I am buying apartment homes and multi-family units each year.

Investing can be risky, but only invest in things that you know, so you are contented when it repays you — **Ralton Thompson**

Value your time frame

How long do you have before you stop working?

If you're far away from your future goals, then you need to start finding additional ways to catch up. We must continue setting targets over time to have a better advantage while the circumstances are changing around us. If you have the amount you "need" in your accounts presently or maybe you can call yourself "economically" independent right now, never get comfortable thinking that is everything is secure. You're still years from retirement or that safe haven you are hankering to create before you die. Stacking up is a smart move but the economies all over the world are always volatile.

If you're closer to your financial goals today, you might have more to lose than to gain in some instances, because stability now becomes just as important as growth. What are you doing with your money to maintain its value? And is your money safe in the banks alone? Knowing all this will give you precedence where your investments need to be and help set the criteria's in moving forward.

Investing for the first time

Investing can be a way of life to some people, and there are a few individuals that somewhat belong to one of these group or schools of thought.

The *Recession Preppers* – these are individuals who believe the financial economy will continue collapsing, so they invest all their money in gold and real estate.

The *Frugal Spenders* – these are people who simply invest in everything to take advantage of the slow and steady increase in the overall value of the markets.

Then we have the *Gambling Day-Traders* – they are often the people you see in real life sitting at their desks, with their walls covered with monitors, flat screen TVs or their phones watching every second of the day to see how the stock market changes.

If you strongly belong to one of these mentioned groups already, then you might not find my investing resources to be too helpful to you. However, if you have an open mind and is interested in learning some simple strategies for successful lifelong investing —then read on.

I can say that I have not found a simple formula to give everyone, because we all have different circumstances, and to say that these are the best path to invest in, would be a lie. But I will say they are some good courses of action you can follow.

Action #1: Start a new saving plan with every additional money you have to invest in short-term, intermediate term or in long-term assets. This can be real estate, existing companies with commodities such as food, gas, and oil or even stocks (if you prefer).

Only buy assets with cash flow or great resale value

What is cash flow?

Cash flow is the total amount of cash or income that an entity receives and disburses during a period. When you have positive cash flow, you have more cash coming into the business than what you have leaving it. If the business has negative cash flow, and it can't afford to make payments on debts, salaries or expand, don't buy, or invest in. The idea of having "enough money to meet your financial obligations" is also known as working capital, and if you're getting money from anything substantially profitable and legal, then use it to buy more.

What is revenue vs. cash flow?

Revenue is the total amount of money going into a business, while cash flow assesses both incoming and outgoing transactions that goes through the account. I told everyone when I started doing this, it had opened up different financial opportunities, but this method only works if you're seeking capital to invest or to buy an asset.

Does buying anything with equity involves risk?

Well as an investor I feel that stocks and cryptocurrency involve a lot more risk. But there is risk attached to every investment product, no matter how good they seem. It's just more pronounced in some cases and not so much in others. But it is best to do more research and find a good product that you understand to invest in.

What is equity?

This is the total liquid cash in value of an asset. This definition may apply to personal or corporate ownership. For example, if you own a car out right, it would be the "current" resale value today, but if you finance a car, it would be amount paid down minus the balance owed on that car loan. So, if a car (the asset) is worth US$20,000 with an outstanding (liability) of US$9,000 then its equity will only be US$11,000.

Note: Total Assets — Total Liabilities = Owner/Shareholders' Equity

In real estate, equity is the difference between the property's current fair market value minus the amount still owed on the mortgage if any. The owner will get the total remaining after selling the property and paying any liens or taxes.

This is also referred to as the "real property value." And if a business or company goes bankrupt and has to liquidate its assets then equity is the amount of money remaining after the business repays its creditors or debts. This is often time called "ownership equity," also known as risk capital or "liable capital."

Invest in Private Equity

If you want to be in the big league early, then private equity is a good start. But this form of investment is typically not accessible for the average investor. Why? because most private equity firms usually look for investors who are willing to commit to as much as US$1 million or more. But in the U.S. some firms have dropped their minimum entry to US$200,000 in recent times, a lot of people might not have that kind of money to invest right now, but it is still an option. Most privately held companies can seek investors by selling off its shares directly in private placements if they decide. These private equity investors can include institutions like insurance companies, pension funds and university endowments, or accredited individuals, if you decide to be one. The accounting equation still applies where the stated equity on the balance sheet is what is left when subtracting *liabilities* from *assets,* giving an estimate of the book value.

Private equity firms are intended to provide investors with profits within a certain timeframe, usually 4-7 years from now. There are other types of Private equity investments that comes into play and at different points during a company's life cycle. Some of which might seem more complicated to the ordinary citizen and to those who simply want to invest for a higher return.

Mainly, it's a new company with no revenue or earnings that can't afford to borrow from a banking institution, so it must get its capital from friends, family members or an individual "investor" like you. I know it would be nice if business funding could simply fall into our laps so we can invest into small businesses or larger companies, right? but the reality is securing funds require diligent work and a lot of preparation.

If you have access to a vast amount of capital right now or you might in the future, funding your entrepreneurial dreams or someone else's can go a far way. Because money doesn't always stretch to as far as we think it will, and we know traditional loans to start a business these days have unwavering prerequisites like credit score requirements and collateral for many individuals.

That is why *crowdfunding* is a growing wealth movement you can be a part of. For those who don't know about crowdfunding, this is when organizations, businesses or individuals put their money together to fund any business idea or project without traditional means. They now have the funding to boost these ventures or to launch any new projects. However, there are drawbacks in every investment, if you are willing to take a risk with 3% to 5% of your investment savings or more, then the potential payoff of investing in private equity could be big, but again, it's not for everyone.

Brand Equity

Investing in a company's goods or services can reap great rewards. But it's better to determine their asset's equity or the influence these businesses or companies' carry. Particularly for larger corporations, it is important to detail these assets, some may include tangible assets, like property, and intangible assets, like the company's reputation and brand identity.

Through the years of establishment and marketing, these companies have developed a customer base, and their brand or image can come to have an ineffaceable value. This value can be seen as "brand equity," which measures the value of the brand, but not the same value as the store-brand version of the product or services.

For example, if you should become a *retailer* or a *wholesaler* of any major brand, let's say of a soft-drink or a wine company, people will buy the most popular brand before buying a store-brand, because they prefer the taste or the more familiar image, right? And if a 4ounce bottle of ketchup (store-brand) costs $1 and the same bottle of ketchup costs $3 but from a major brand, then the "brand equity" is $2. This is considered the difference in value over another product. So chose your investments wisely if you're investing in brand equity.

There is also a negative side to brand equity, where hurtful publicity can occur due to damage goods, terrible customer service and product recalls or a disaster, but this comes with every business territory.

Action #2: Be a private money lender, yes, you can be your own bank. Private money lending is when a private individual or a small business lends another investor, party, or company their own personal funds to use for investment purposes. It is an alternative option for financing outside of a traditional bank or lending institution. But you must budget the amount of money you want to lend, do up the legal binding documents and carryout the credible background checks on these borrowers before you go into business. Plus, if you expect any major expenses in the next year or two, keep enough money for those unexpected repayments or delays just in case things go badly.

Action #3: Put your money towards tangible assets with cash flow — this is anything that holds value over time and that is in your possession, such as real estate, equipment and certain businesses are all tangible investments.

Wealth Preservation with long-term tangible investments

Real Estate

Use up any equity invested in a home, multi-family unit or a condo

Everyone could agree that all we need some place to live and most of us will start out with renting an apartment or buying a home at some point. Years ago, I learnt that real estate is the best long-term structure to have in my possession and it is by far my top best tangible investment to own. Whether you're looking to buy or rent-to-own in areas that have low income or vying for the ones in the upscale communities, this still works. The type of properties you desire to buy will either increase in value or go down based on location. But as long as you're receiving cash flow from rents, don't focus too much on the property's value. You should only care about the value of the property when you decide to sell it at the end of that holding period.

If you should buy lower priced investment homes in lesser socio-economic neighborhoods, sometimes you are faced with higher management fees and more maintenance issues, mainly because those neighborhoods have the older types of homes. One ray of hope is that these tenants may still be able to afford and continue paying the rent during certain economic times. But it's wise to make sure your tenants are comprised of people who are employed in somewhat of a stable job field or with government funded programs. Otherwise, you can end up with many evictions and subsequent vacancies.

If you understand how home equity works, then you will know that it can be a great source to use when purchasing or buying other assets of value. But first you must either own a property or you are in the process of purchasing one. Your intentions should be using it for "cash-flow" or a side business. So, the amount of equity one has in their residence or property represents how much of the asset they entirely own, simply by subtracting the mortgage owed or the debt remaining.

For example, if you own a home with a mortgage on it. And say the house has a current market value of US$250,000 and the mortgage owed total is US$150,000. Then you would have had a US$100,000 worth of equity in the home. And this will keep increasing as time goes by. Home equity can be an individual's greatest source of collateral, and the owner can use it to get a what some call a second mortgage or a home-equity line of credit to buy another investment property for cash flow.

Real Estate is vulnerable to civic unrest, but still sustainable in a crisis.

I chose to invest in residential real estate because as a landlord/manager we may escape some economic variances better than other real estate investors in the commercial world. There are many other avenues to make money in real estate, such as acquisitions, wholesaling, construction development and deed investing, etc. But people will always need a place to live and not all businesses can stay open.

We have seen what civic unrest as done to major city services because of unplanned events. Making commercial spaces empty or abandon in recent times, even when rental houses are vacated in the cities, tenants will still move to the suburbs and utilities for some commercial spaces are useless with no revenue until things are restored. Minimal rents might be collected during this period, but owning real estate as never decreased its value because of these unsteady events.

Can I buy collectible items to hold value?

When I talk about investing in collectible items, this can include cars, toys, games, rare coins, books and even the fine arts. These are just some of the safer investments to start out with. But heck, all investments are still risky, right? You always want to start out small before you jump big; because I had to learn the hard way believe me. Some collectible items will be more costly at the start, but they usually bring in more value at the end. Keep in mind, not all collectible items can or will hold their value for a long period, sometimes they get devalued sooner rather later, so be prepared to sell your collections when the time seems right to sell.

In my research I read that over 70% of collectors said that investing was the reason behind their decision to purchase collectibles after the stock market crash in 2008. Now I realize that bad things will have to happen before most people do anything good about it, and it doesn't always mean it will change everything either. When investing into anything or anyone, ensure that the determining factors are ones that you are comfortable with regardless of the outcome. So, if investing into collectibles is a resourceful way to exercise your knowledge and interest in a product and it doesn't give you any profit in the end, still enjoy it for what it is.

What is the downside to investing in Collectibles?

Collectibles have a more difficult market to track for one, so where and how to store collectibles can be an issue at times, also knowing the best way for collectibles to be compared to other types of investments is another uncertainty. The biggest question I get sometimes from my friends is what exactly should I invest in? Or what collectible items must I buy? It is important to research any investment to determine what exactly you are investing in first, then ensure you are aware of the potential resale value it may have.

Because most collectibles don't necessarily appreciate with time as other investments do, it might not be profitable to some investors who want that assurance and a big pay out after all the work. We must understand that the marketplace is simple, but different and someone can be willing to pay a high price for a particular collectible today, but it ends up undervalued tomorrow for some reason. However, the method behind determining the value is usually at a specific *time* and the *demand* for the product, and not because it was popular.

Overall, diversifying your portfolio in different tangible investments may be a way to protect your net worth during troubling economic times. Collectibles will often become more profitable when the dollar is *weak*. But I believe your major returns will come from the best investments that you love the most and surrounding yourself with great people who can help you find these high valued ventures to be a part of.

Finding the Right Sources when buying assets

Take this advice very well; it is worth the time to think about what you truly want from all your investments. For example, don't pay retail price when buying a residential or commercial properties and expect to sell them for a bigger return in a shorter space of time. The same thing goes for equipment, consumer products and any other investment for that matter. Buying low means you're going to seek out the most reasonable wholesale sources and prices, and the best way to start is by doing your homework and your due diligence first. Your best prices will come from primary dealers, auctions, and emotional sellers. Most secondary dealers sometimes will buy from other wholesalers (usually the primary ones) and then resell them, still the main intention is to buy way below retail margin, if possible.

Today it's way easier to find good sources for any investment venture or platform to buy on or trade from with so many available products. There you have both primary and secondary dealers that are accessible.

Most people start with the internet, trade magazines, the local directory and then the marketing agencies who floods the billboards and posters with their listings. If you're knowledgeable you can find other marketplaces around your community or hometown and get the best deals on anything that you're interested in. You just have to look long enough to see them.

Wherever there is big money or profits to be made, always be wary of the fraudsters, Ponzi dealers and scammers lurking around. Most waiting for a quick fortune from people who are desperate and gullible. And it is only natural, so treat everything with respect, qualify each investment thoroughly and don't always be fool by anything too good to be true.

Action #4: Consider buying cash value Life Insurance

Another divisive investment strategy many would not consider is cash value life insurance. The reason I have suggested it as an investment option is the fact that this kind of life insurance product does not only pay out a death benefit to your beneficiaries, but it also allows you to accumulate *value* with an investment portion from your payments before you pass away. There are two types of cash value insurance offered in the United States and they are whole life and universal life. Term life insurance is mainly popular and by far the cheaper option for most people, but it only covers your death. In some countries there might be different insurance investments available, but it is wise to do your own research depending on where you live and see what options are offered in your region.

If you are deciding between a term life and cash value life insurance policy, one of the biggest variances to look on is the investment portion offered by the cash value policy. If you want both, then that's a plus, to the best of knowledge and to date, there are no legal limits as to how many life insurance policies you can own.

If you are not in the financial position right now, it is still advisable to get one soon, however these options I leave to your own devise. From a business perspective the cash value policy offers the tax advantages to your investment. Consumers have reported over the years that whole life policies are a very costly way to invest for the future. But in some cases that cost may be worth the benefits in the long run.

One of the best perks of using cash value life insurance is for accrued value that can be borrowed against like a loan throughout your life and it doesn't get hit with *income tax* and who likes paying taxes on every dollar they make anyway? I sure know I don't. And while cash value life insurance isn't for everyone, it is still one of the resourceful way the rich and wealthy pass on high net worth to their children and avoid the high

Advantages of Cash Value Life Insurance

Tax-Sheltered Growth

The invested cash value portion from the insurance policy will now grow tax-free if the money stays in your account. As an example, say you have a cash value policy that you invest into bonds that pays you interest right? These same bonds you own are in a brokerage account, you then pay taxes on the interest gained each year from these bonds.

But in a cash value insurance policy, you don't pay taxes on the interest, as long as you don't cash out more than the amount you've paid in premiums, you can withdraw the money tax-free, so you can still win, you just can't win in everything.

Unlimited Renewability

If you decide to carry a life insurance for the rest of your life, the cash value policy can be a good investment in my view, a lot of times we worry about fees incurred from any investment, but most businesses live off fees to give service to others and pay salaries and other things, we can't always think small, because not spending money doesn't always prevent you from losing it to something else. If you take out a cash value policy, your premiums are fixed, so if you keep paying your premiums, your policy will never be canceled no matter how long you live. While on the other hand, *term life* insurance is only good for a certain period. Once that period ends and you're still alive, your policy is no more and you're not getting anything.

Disadvantages of Buying Cash Value Life Insurance

High Fees

Cash value life insurance policies are infamous for high fees, yes; it can be disheartening because the commissions can run high in the first year, according to experts in the field. In addition, your annual fees can go up with your account value. Unless you are a high-income earner who has maxed out retirement account contributions and want an additional account for tax-deferred savings, then this option can work.

Also, many policies include a surrender fee, which reduces the amount of cash value you get to keep, usually within a certain period if you decide to cash out your policy, which can go up to 10 years.

But I am not an expert, still talk to a financial advisor about the expected amount of time for your policy.

Death Benefit Limitations

When you build up cash value in your policy, you are normally allowed to borrow against it. However, as profitable as it might be to borrow against the value of your life insurance, you might be unthinkingly limiting the death benefit for your beneficiaries on that policy: now if you are borrowing for a good cause that can be great, but if anything should happen before you pay it back, any outstanding balance on that loan will reduce the full amount that your beneficiaries would receive. For example, you have a US$300,000 death benefit, if you die before with a US$85,000 outstanding loan balance on the policy, your beneficiaries will only get US$215,000.

When is cash value life insurance a wise investment?

This can be a good investment if you can afford the higher premiums. But when you are reviewing life insurance options, I would advise you to take into question the sizeable premium that comes with these cash value life insurance policies. I believe in some countries outside of the United States, cash value life insurance policies may not be available. But if you have saved up enough for retirement and may want to invest some of your money in a less risky venture, then I would consider this is an option if it's available.

On the other hand, some believe that it's better to "buy term and invest the rest." This route means you can take advantage of the lower premium on a term life insurance policy, which is for a set for a time (typically up 10-20plus years). And then invest the cost you would pay for a cash value life insurance into a savings account or in the stock market, etc. But these options are always there to choose from, just choose one that will work best for you.

Action #5: Choose investments that match your endurance for risk.

Investing must always involve asking where do I really want to put my money? And how do I start with the income I have? These answers will also depend on your goals and your willingness to take on more risk, in exchange for a higher potential reward. Most people are rushing these days to buy up stocks and the new trending phenomena *cryptocurrency and NFT's*. This has become the favorite new form of equity for traders and most new investors. But as many may know these investments can be very volatile over a shorter-term period, historically we have seen that holding certain assets for longer periods can decrease the risk of loss over time.

Whereas in today's day and age you can virtually use technology to be certain of the performance of a stock portfolio outperforming of a bond, mutual fund, and cash portfolio, but if we are using history as our guide, you must ensure your risk tolerance is up to par if you should lose money. So, ask yourself again, can you trust cryptocurrencies and NFT's? And should you jump into the world of crypto investing? Always do your research and seek out the right resources to decide for yourself.

History does unusual things sometimes, so it should not be our only guide! Now if you have money sitting on that you don't need until the next 12 to18 years then it could be invested into a long-term producing asset or assets. It might not be all in stocks, cryptocurrencies, NFT's or bonds, etc. Because you can never be too sure of when you might want your money out of these risky investments or other non-liquid assets, even if history says you should. Only invest a percentage of your money that you are comfortable with and keep the rest in something safer.

Chapter 18

How Taxes Can Affect Investment Returns

You must understand how interest income from your investments is taxable and seek out "lawful" alternatives on how to lower it if you want to keep most of your money.

In the United States the Internal Revenue Service says all income you make both earned and unearned from your job, your business and from your investments is deemed taxable. So, whether it includes interest income that is originated through banks or brokerage accounts, gambling, lawsuit settlements and from certain assets, like stocks, bonds or mutual funds, the IRS wants a piece of it. These interests on the money from any type of income or certain investments, is also taxable on the state and federal level. But you can avoid or defer the taxes on interest earned in tax-advantaged accounts and with certain income assets available to you. The realization we all must face is that no matter how cunning and savvy we all can be, paying income taxes and other taxes is a way of life anywhere in the world and it will continue to be so until we die.

What is interest income?

Interest income is the amount paid out to an entity or individual for lending them their money or allowing another entity to use the funds in return for a profit. On another scale, interest income is the amount earned by an investor's money that he places in an investment asset, account, or a project. These include Checking and Savings accounts, US Savings and Treasury bonds, Certificates of Deposit (CDs), Corporate bonds, Mutual funds/ETFs, Money Market accounts, various loans made to others and income from pass-through businesses, such as partnerships or S-corporations.

Is there any interest income or income tax that is free?

Fortunately, yes, and no. In the U.S. only one major type of asset is deemed feasible to produce this non-taxable interest income: and these are municipal bonds (also called "munis") and private activity bonds, which are still taxable under the alternative minimum tax (AMT) regulated by the tax system.

These bonds are issued by states, counties, cities, and other government agencies which help fund major projects, such as building airports, public schools and hospitals, highways, and other civic buildings. If these bonds are issued by your home state, then the interest income it provides is also free from state and local income taxes, along with municipal bond funds, which are tax-exempt from federal taxes.

Fun fact: Municipal bonds are also classified as "triple-tax-exempt" bonds which are tax-free from federal, state, and local taxes.

Note: There are only a few states in the U.S. that don't tax your earned income which includes — Alaska, Florida, New Hampshire, Nevada, South Dakota, Texas, Tennessee, Washington, and Wyoming to date. But New Hampshire, on the other hand taxes all interest-income and dividends, according to the Tax Foundation. Tennessee has now eliminated its taxes on investment income in 2021. But all these tax benefits can always change in the future, so while you are increasing your income over time, still try to protect it from being taxed heavily anywhere you are.

Can relocating to another country or moving to other states with no income tax be beneficial?

Yes, but also no, there are right reasons why moving to another state or outside your home country can be good, but NOT to avoid taxes! Many people today still think that dodging taxes will be beneficial to them in the long run, and it's actually the opposite.

While it can be good for people with higher earnings, more job opportunities, and other reasons. *Relocating will be more valuable to you and your family as a unit.* If you don't make high income, then paying no income tax is less helpful, because there are ways to get back high tax returns if you are using a well-versed CPA that knows the tax system.

These states or other countries without income tax still need tax revenue, and they will get that money through other taxes, such as sales and property taxes. So as a general rule always consider your best options. Aside from your income concerns, don't get disquietude if you are subjected to an income tax or state taxes.

If you are being doubled taxed this can be for several reasons, one, you still live in another state or another country that does tax your income there, and two, you are still regarded as a resident or a citizen living and working outside. It can also go for your business that you make money from, even if it is in another state or region. So, every income of a sizeable amount usually gets reported to the tax services one way or another.

How will the tax rate affect my interest income?

With interest income it doesn't have a special tax rate like how the profits from your investments are taxed. You pay the taxes on the interest as if it was ordinary income, that is, the same rate as your other income you make, like your wages or self-employment earnings.

Interest income can also be subject to another tax called the *Net Investment Income Tax (NIIT).* Typically, it is all your investment income that comes from (interest, capital gains, dividends, even distributions from annuities, and the income from passive activities, rents, and royalties) then subtracting any related investment expenses classified by the IRS.

Who pays Net Investment Income Tax?

The net investment income tax applies to all taxpayers who are U.S. citizens or residents that has an appreciable amount of investment income, typically high-net-worth families and individuals with noticeable assets living in or outside the country.

Is there any way to avoid taxes on interest income or lower it?

I believe it is very hard to avoid paying taxes on your interest income, but it's not impossible; I will list a few strategies I think you can use to lower it, especially with assets that generate a lot of income. But I will advise you as Warren Buffet said, "Invest in what you know...and nothing more."

One of the easiest ways to avoid bad investment decisions, is NOT getting involved in ones that are overly complex for you.

Use charitable contributions as a tax advantage

A lot of people may not know they're able to reduce their net investment income through charitable contributions, yes, and it's 100% legal. If you decide to make charitable donations in the future using publicly traded securities like stocks, bonds, exchange-traded funds (ETFs) and mutual funds, held over a year are more, you can earn a tax deduction for the donated amounts which would lower your tax bill, and it is a great feeling to give a percentage of your earnings towards a worthy cause.

Cash donations are usually the first proclivity for some individuals, but giving with non-cash assets (like stocks, bonds, exchange-traded funds (ETFs) and mutual funds) is a more fruitful strategy that can increase both the amount of money you give to a tax-exempt non-profit organization and your tax savings at the same time. In donating any appreciated stock, your capital gains then vanishes entirely and don't have to be reported on your taxes, allowing you to permanently avoid any long-term gains tax liability that you would owe otherwise in the future. However, this gnomic method is now being scrutinized by the IRS and can possibly change in the future.

In different parts of the world, giving to a charitable cause can influence a lot of change, and some organizations will take cash donations preferably, while others can accept appreciated non-cash assets (these are regarded as the tax-smart charitable gifts in the U.S.).

Not all charities can accept them, because they do not have the structure setup to receive these gifts unfortunately. Only public charities called *Donor-advised fund,* that are 501(c)(3) non-profits which have these resources and expertise for evaluating, receiving, and liquidating these assets, but do your research to see if this tax advantage will benefit you.

Another charity advantage you can consider is *a charitable remainder trust* (CRT) to reduce NIIT liability. "A CRT is an irrevocable, tax-exempt trust in which the grantor places assets to provide income during a specific period. CRTs are exempt from Section 1411 of the U.S. tax code that applies to the NIIT, which means that gains sold by the CRT won't be subject to the net investment income tax. However please consult with a tax or legal advisor on these matters because gifts of appreciated non-cash assets can involve complicated tax analysis and advanced planning, due to changes that will happen every year in the economy.

Some loopholes on how you can pay no tax on gains and other investments

Investors who are experienced in stock trading for a number of years have been highly successful because they understand the game. As an individual who pays taxes, I've learnt that any huge profit you make from the stock market must be reported to the IRS in tax season, less you know what will happen if you don't. But what millions of American taxpayers don't know is that there is a provision in the U.S. tax laws that let you sell stocks at a profit without having to pay any income tax on it. But this strategy must be executed properly, and you must keep up to date to see if you qualify.

Think long term to get the tax authorities off your back

As a taxpayer you must develop a long-term investing mindset, so you can benefit from the IRS or the Tax authorities anywhere in the world. You may be asking why? because the lawmakers everywhere created certain tax laws for the sapient individuals to benefit on long-term investment holdings versus profits on shorter-term investments. Those who don't understand how these tax systems work, has a different tax treatment under the law.

Be aware that under the current tax law, U.S. taxpayers get a tax break if they hold onto a stock or an investment for one year or longer, this could change, and it might not. So, if you sell a stock or investment under one year, then you'll pay whatever the ordinary income tax rate is on any profits from that sale. But if you hold onto it and sell it after, then you'll get a lower tax rate.

This goes for everyone with returns on long-term capital gains, both in the highest tax bracket and those in the lowest tax brackets as well. With the current tax incentives under the law, it allows these individuals with the lowest income of them all, to pay no tax whatsoever on their long-term capital gains, but this can also change in the near future.

Make use of it or lose all of it

When you are a high-income earner or an investor, you will pretty much pay more taxes than regular individuals, because you possess more than the average person, so keep in mind that your taxable income will include profits from investment sales or gains from stocks if you sold them. And this is if they are reported accordingly to the tax instructions. If you made more in long-term capital gains that took you over the income threshold; then it's still not as bad paying tax on the excess that you made, versus what you would pay on the ordinary income rate. Because this lowers the tax hit than a regular taxpayer would get instead.

To use the approach, all you have to do is to sell your stock or the asset for a profit. Say you do this; you can then buy it back at the same time with the hopes of seeing a bigger return on the gains. But these strategies you must do a lot of research on; I repeatedly tell everyone this to ensure they know what their options are, to better reduce their taxes at the end of the tax year. And if you decide to, please review each strategy that is available to save you money, and to avoid higher taxes down the road or if any at all.

Should I invest outside of my home country?

Ask yourself, do I love traveling and exploring different cultures outside of my own country? If your answer is yes, then having an offshore bank account can be a fulfilling start for those who are bold and brave to do it.

What's more exclusive to you is having an offshore account as an investment vehicle to grow your business and to make your trips overseas worthwhile. In the world of offshore banking, there is a great deal of misinformation floating around. But this experience is one I am excited to share that most people will not find in their domestic banking systems. Not only does offshore bank accounts benefit individuals overseas, but it is also a proactive means of protection and convenience for offshore businesses to conduct trade legally, while investing in foreign markets.

There always conventional ways how to make serious money without paying a lot of taxes but be smart about it, not evasive.

Why should I open an offshore bank account if my funding resources are limited?

This investment move will not be for you if you are not currently in the position to do so; it is more geared towards a wealthy individual, who sees the benefits of using an offshore bank account for these rewarding benefits.

Better Tax Advantages

When you have amassed a certain amount of wealth in your home country, the high taxation will make you be hesitant to put more money in a bank account to be declared the tax authorities. In comparison to opening an offshore bank account in certain tax havens, this allows the account holder to be entitled to a favorable tax rate, which can either lower the taxes or even have no tax rate at all.

For this recourse, most companies go offshore just to optimize the tax benefits outside of their home headquarters.

Growth for Future Planning

There is so much uncertainty with the future of any economy and planning ahead is always the best reserve you can have. In recent times opening offshore bank accounts as become an increasing nuisance for some individuals who want to genuinely invest for the right reasons. Due to the crack down on money laundering, fraud and other illegitimate use offshore bank accounts, many countries have adopted oversight measures like the Common Reporting Standard (CRS) and FATCA (Foreign Account Tax Compliance Act).

As of April 1, 2017, over 113 countries have signed an Intergovernmental Agreement (IGA) or have reached "agreements in substance" with the U.S. to comply with FATCA. And now more than 180,000 financial institutions have registered with the IRS. So don't think you will be hiding all your assets entirely from Uncle Sam (U.S.A).

The interest returns are higher

If you value the profits that can be made from high yielding accounts, then keeping some of your money in an offshore bank can offer higher interest rates than those in your home country. But buy assets in that that country for continual high interest return, it is better to set up a long-term account to achieve this. People will offer a lot of different advice when it comes to the best offshore bank accounts. And it doesn't mean they are necessarily wrong. Many countries offer different options for different purposes. So, there is not one perfect banking country for one person or a company, because each one serves a different agenda for one another.

Currency diversification

It is vital to keep retaining your wealth in an ever-changing economy. And offshore banking enables account holders to have a diverse currency portfolio in their offshore accounts. Think of all the currencies you possible own that will have a great buying value? And put these different currencies to use that you can make multi-currency transactions as well. In this way your assets won't be affected so easily by currency fluctuations that are often seen in your home country.

Account Privacy

Another great benefit of offshore banking is privacy laws that many offshore banks have enacted to accommodate stricter corporate and banking confidentiality under their jurisdictions. All this is to put a higher emphasis on the account holder's needs, allowing their information to be kept safe and nonpublic. Only the relevant authorities have claims to such information, and any other entities outside of these laws will be deemed as criminal offenders and violators, which their actions can lead to serious consequences for penalty or even imprisonment. An example of such high-profile banking privacy is the Swiss offshore bank account.

Convenience you must consider

How safe is your money though? Think about it? Can you always access it from anywhere? If you want to be sure of anything when traveling, then an having less cash in a bank account is a good idea to consider. They have the convenience of around-the-clock service regardless of where you are living or the time zone you are in. And if you are an individual who loves traveling, then an offshore bank account is easily accessible from anywhere in the world. But ensure there is adequate service for the account choice you are considering.

This includes but not limited to, 24/7 internet banking, debit or credit card access, ATMs networks and other services. You may ask yourself why would do I need this information? Because the purpose of this is to edify and expand your knowledge on how money works internationally and from different purview.

What are the investment opportunities?

A huge plus for offshore banking is that account holders can access a wide variety of investments and funding opportunities with less government intrusion. In some countries there are regulations and laws that do restrict the foreign investment opportunities for their residents, and this is where you can come in and make a difference. These flexible investment options can attract entrepreneurs, investors, and bankers with unlimited choices to reach international markets in the interim.

The importance of security

Offshore accounts do offer a level of security, which is an attractive facet for many offshore account holders. Research as shown, there has been millions of lawsuits filed in the United States each year for breach of security on individual assets, accounts, and personal information. But this does not mean it won't happen to you outside of your home country.

There is this uncertainty and unfavorable condition with every economy. Some people usually abuse a system they think they understand in their home country, usually it results in seizures of assets, high inflation from external factors, loss of investments due to bad decisions, high numbers in bankruptcy and other financial deficit through this exposure.

So having other assets in other accounts or in other investments elsewhere can be more beneficial if this should happen. Try to ask where is the best place to keep my money to buy assets in case something should happen? There is a lot of options out there, yes, but always consider them all. Many offshore banks are very renowned and productively operated under strict jurisdictions. With full intent to offer the highest level of security where depositors' money is concern because they need your business.

Keynote: Do not be discouraged if there are certain misusages of these offshore accounts connected to money laundering, illegal tax evasion, or criminal behaviors. Always make use of any monetary advantage of offshore banking as long as it's totally legal and can benefit you and your family in the future.

Be cautious of who you invest money with

Most people who invest any substantial amount of cash always want a higher return on their investments. But understand that if something sounds too good to be true, then it probably is. I have loss thousands of dollars on investments that I was hasty to do and didn't do my research on in the past. And there are some deals I've gotten a less desirable return on, but the point is, be thorough and be sure of what you are investing in. While there are a number of great reasons to get an offshore bank account, you may never need one at all. If you are happy in your home country and have no desire to travel outside or leave, then you shouldn't over-extend yourself in any overseas accounts just for the sake of having them. However, if you are contemplating in becoming an international citizen, starting global business, or just broadening your wealth, then getting an offshore bank account is a part of the first step.

Try to look for developing markets as an investor

If you have the potential to be a diverse investor, then looking to grow within developing markets is another windfall you can possess, if you go about it the right way. Draft up a list and then visit these areas, or even these countries where you can find vast number of equities to invest in, but make sure you study these markets well.

In most developing markets with large equities, they normally bring out a wide scope of opportunities that needs funding or assistance. From revenue to be invested in infrastructure, roads, education even areas with foreign currencies to fund new and current local businesses. But not all markets have these opportunities to bring up high profits if any, sometimes your money or the asset you have is only a ray of hope for some in a struggling cause that just need the financial support.

Investments in these developing markets can attract individuals like you who want to make a difference, and not only for the money or wealth, but if you are helping to grow economies with your engine. A large majority of people can get to move out of poverty, resulting in a growth of the middle class and who doesn't want that? You can bring in new ideas or creativeness of economic development with little funding that can go a far way, and this could drive economic growth to innovate and prosper cities, states and countries down the road.

Takeaway: Developing markets can be very unstable but also promising because they come with both risks and rewards. *Preparation and research proves the best action for the unknown,* but access to different markets and countries can offer discovery of new wealth that many investors seek to grow and diversify.

How are you planning to leave your wealth to your family? And do have an estate plan?

When you hear the word "estate," many things come to mind such as land, property, and other large investments, but an estate actually entails way more personal and business assets on a whole. The planning is where you make a collective list of legal documents that will protect your assets and personal holdings, to outturn the details of how you want them to be pass down or distributed. Creating a will is good, but it's not everything. An estate plan can arrange your affairs and finances if anything should happen to you, and in some cases, while you're still alive.

How to get started with estate planning

1. Create a list of all your financial holdings, personal property, against the liabilities to total your net worth.

2. Determine or make changes to your beneficiaries to explain who should receive money from any life insurance policies, annuities, retirement accounts, and other financial accounts, etc.

3. Ensure you seek well accredited financial advisors who can refer you to qualified estate planning attorneys or firms to assist you.

4. Always revisit your estate plan regularly, no matter how contented you may seem.

THE UNUSUAL PATH TO SUCCESS

Ways to protect your inheritance from taxes

Protecting your inheritances is like preserving your lifeline, but there is a growing social opinion from others who don't have this privilege like some do. And they think these people should become wealthy by working hard for it, rather than inheriting this wealth from their families or relatives.

From this notion many governments impose significant inheritance taxes, also known as "death taxes." But in some countries like Canada, Singapore, Macau, Mexico, New Zealand, and Australia to date, do not charge any inheritance taxes.

The United States does not consider receipt of an inheritance as taxable income for federal or state tax purposes. However, any future earnings on these inherited assets are taxable, unless it comes from a tax-free source. Always remember the tax authorities know about any inherited asset you receive, and if you gain any interest income on them, they want to know, why? Because everybody wants a share of the profits, and they have regulatory bodies keeping watch somewhere or everywhere.

Consider putting your inheritance into a trust

It is wise to make a well-calculated decision to control any inheritance you might receive, and for that reason know the importance of each asset type and understand where it's coming from, so you can be prepared for any income tax concern for each category. Typically, you can think of inherited assets in these groups:

1. Cash and Securities
2. Real Estate
3. Life Insurance and Annuities
4. Retirement Accounts
5. Art and Collectibles
6. Interests in Trust

Not everyone will want to preserve their wealth in a *trust*, but if you are expecting an inheritance from your parents or other relatives even from friends, I would suggest they set up a trust to *apportion* these assets. A trust allows anyone to pass on assets to their beneficiaries after death and this is without having to go through court and administration of estate.

It might be easier and simpler for parents to just put their assets into joint name accounts with their children, but this can actually increase the taxes the children will pay later on.

In most cases when an account holder dies, the joint holder inherits not only the assets, but also the *cost basis*, and if there is a tax entity that mandates this rule in your country or region, they will use it to figure out the asset's taxable gain over the years and its current market value. And this can get a significant tax hit if and when the beneficiary sells the asset in any event.

You may be asking if a will is similar to a trust? Yes, but is a will better? Well, I wouldn't really agree. Trusts traditionally avoid interference from the state and other associated expenses that comes. If you decide to pursue this route in setting up a trust, I would implore you to fixate your priorities, and your wishes for the assets in a revocable trust and you having 100% control and not the lawyer or professional advisor. So, you the grantor(s) can take the assets out if you deem it necessary. But with an irrevocable trust it generally binds the assets until you the grantor(s) pass away, this way the terms cannot be amended, modified, or terminated without permission from the beneficiaries you have selected. Others will advise you differently, but always ensure you are not coerced in to doing something you do not understand.

Give away some of the inheritance, whether large or small

Am I asking you to give away some of your wealth? Yes, you darn right! In *Acts 20:35* NKJV, Paul says, *"I have shown you in every way, by laboring like this, that you must support the weak. And remember the words of the Lord Jesus, that He said, 'It is more blessed to give than to receive.'* Many might not agree with this sound doctrine, but it is more noble and satisfying to help others who are in need, than to let taxes benefit more out of your inheritance.

Sometimes your wealth will increase just by giving a portion of it to others. While on the other hand you can potentially offset any taxable gains from your inheritance, with tax deductions when you give to charitable organizations. If you're expecting to leave money to people when you die, consider giving it as annual gifts to your beneficiaries while you're still alive, because the dead can't take anything with them.

You can give a certain amount to each person without being subject to gift taxes and this depends how the tax laws are setup in your home country. But as always, please speak with an estate planning professional just to ensure you're making the right decisions with any estate affairs.

Keep track of your estate while it is growing

The wealthier you become through the years, the more convoluted your estate gets. As the saying goes, "more money, more problems." So, the best way to grow your estate is to carefully track your wealth through a structured system with professional assistance or with other free personal finance tools that can be used on a laptop or a mobile phone. Staying on top of your possessions will lessen your headaches and disorganization when it comes around to tax season.

How do most Millionaires and Billionaires avoid high estate taxes?

This might come as a surprised but it's not a secret, that multi-millionaires and billionaires avoid paying estate taxes simply because they learn how the system of wealth works and then they plan properly over time. The United States as a current estate tax exemption-threshold with a set limit per person and after that limit is exceeded; every dollar over that is passed down, is taxed at a set percentage rate.

The hidden knowledge of how America's wealthiest families create empires and pay less estate tax is through what they call a *Grantor Retained Annuity Trust,* or GRAT. In some countries this might be called another financial vehicle to pay fewer taxes on luxuriant amount of wealth. If a GRAT is setup properly and administered with the favorable conditions, then a significant amount of wealth can be passed on to the next generation with practically no estate or gift tax ramification.

But how does this work for wealthy people to save on estate taxes?

To explain this in the simplest way, when you are worth millions or billions of dollars, your estate will far exceed the tax exemption limit on estate taxes. As a result, setting up a GRAT is what most wealthy people do, but not all.

Earlier in the chapter you have heard me mentioned trusts more than once and it is for several reasons. When you, the grantor, transfer these appreciating assets to a trust (suitably a GRAT) you *retain* the right as the name suggests, in receiving an annuity payment for a number of years as termed or a lifetime of the trust. At the end of the period, these remaining assets in the GRAT are then distributed to your heirs or other beneficiaries as desired, to protect the assets in the lineage.

As you know, there are pros and cons with every trust, but it is ensuring that you know, rather than you don't. The great thing wealthy families'

197

love about this trust is when you transfer assets into a GRAT it eventually triggers a gift tax classification, without having to pay any gift taxes.

However, pay attention when you see the value of the taxable gift amount of the assets, because it's not the amount being reflected, compared to what was transferred into the GRAT originally.

Instead, the gift is "reduced" by the actuarial value of the annuity you retain. Make sense? If not, you'll get it eventually. If this estate strategy is structured properly, the annuity would equal the value of the assets, and there is no gift. This is referred to as a "zeroed-out" GRAT. There are other features of this trust, but I only chose to mention one. So again, this is a huge benefit for wealthier individuals or families with large estates.

Note: if you pass away before the term expires, then all assets in the trust is then returned to you and is once again included in your taxable estate. Remember I said you must develop a long-term mindset when investing or planning for the future, because this allows more time for your assets to appreciate and lowering a high capital gain to avoid taxes. This is the main motivator behind establishing a GRAT in the first place.

Avoiding high estate taxes with a business

Many business owners are mainly focused on the day-to-day affairs in operating their business. And thinking about estate taxes is not regularly at the forefront of their brains. Typically, a lot of individuals everywhere just think about taxes at tax time and not throughout the entire year, leaving estate and inheritance taxes to have significant effects on a family business.

Most of the super-wealthy people in the world are business owners. Some either own significant amount of equity in their own business or others have equity in other businesses as investors. To start using any business to lower estate taxes, first seek out a business partner or an associate who want to start up a business or invest in a startup company that needs capital.

Lesson: Build businesses or build your own equity with fruitful ventures, because from these investments you can become wealthy and leave generational assets.

This can either work for you or it might not, all investments are risky, so you must determine what kind of contracts or structural investment to put in place, from this your heirs or successors can be partial owners of the business. Along these lines they can reap some of the profits that will ultimately come to fruition and reduce the value of your estate and giving them a stake in the business. I believe if you invest wisely over time, you can even get to a billionaire status, allowing 70% of your wealth to come from business investments alone.

A financial review for the future

I hope after completing this chapter on investing and tax planning that your wealth journey might be more translucent than before, because building and sustaining wealth is not easy. And I can assure you that if it was easy, then everybody would be doing it, plain and simple.

A question that many people might be facing today is how can I improve my earnings for the future? And will my current finances be in order to make it through the next two years or more? You might be thinking how can I move forward financially while the future still seem so uncertain? Well, the truth is the future doesn't need to be clear for you to take meaningful action, you must research, plan, and go for it if you want to build and protect your assets.

Wherever you are in the world, working or just earning money by all legal means, try to save towards a goal or a dream, this will be your investment. Keep track of everything to know your spending wisely, because you don't want to be penny-wise and pound foolish out here. Only a small percentage of people will ever have to worry about these issues of earning and protecting wealth, because sadly enough not everyone will want to sacrifice the things that come from working and creating this dynasty, to last for generations to come, I say this to you, try to be the first, and not the last.

Chapter 19

What is the Final Goal?

"It always seems impossible until it's done."
—Nelson Mandela *(Former President of South Africa)*

In this chapter I share my final views on how you can build success daily, but all this experience will only benefit you if you decide to use it and advance in your personal and professional life.

A personal objective is important for everything you do, so always tailor your *wants* separately from your *needs*. This way you are setting up yourself to get the best out of every situation, and not because you deserve it, but it's from the work you've done. Sadly, not everything good will always be offered to you in life, nevertheless we shouldn't abandon our dreams or aspirations. The Great King Solomon had many regrets throughout his life even though *God* gave him everything on earth he could possibly wish for. Even with every experience he had known to men and unlimited wisdom, he was still not happy in the end. Your goals should not be getting famous or being rich anywhere in the world. It should be gaining personal and financial success at anything you desire, because this will make room for you to solve the problems in the world.

Come Prepared, but Expect the Unexpected

When it comes to preparation for most people whether to pitch their service, their products or even their ideas, they fumble or blow their chance at the opportunity, I too have fallen victim to this many times, so don't think I was perfect.

To be a top producer and a performer, always plan ahead even when it doesn't seem important. Use your time to create concise, memorable, and powerful pitches to communicate your value with transparency and conviction. It's like practicing every day until you out-beat your own self. Nobody knew I used to interview myself with every possible question I think any interviewer could ask me, I would sit at my office desk alone for hours just doing this. You may find yourself in an *unusual* position someday to pitch your plan or an idea when you least expect it, it can be at your workplace, on the street, in a restaurant or on the bus, you name it. And you may only get a few seconds or a minute to make it resonate and stick, so be prepared and be ready.

How do I get people to remember me (or my company)?

The heart of any personal branding should be focused around cultivating what no one else has ever seen, and that is becoming a *benchmark*, be that standard and not the standard of someone else's. We should not only strive to be the best in our chosen line of work or profession but be the prototype in it. For example, if you are a teacher, a life coach, an engineer, a developer, or a manager, then be the best professional in town and online. Stamp that level of value on yourself that you always stand out and everything else will follow.

Be noticeable without seeking attention, if you do not crave for the instant gratification of anything, then you will be humbled to manage your growth over time. This will not be easy for many people, but let your work be a reflection of who you are, that everyone ties it directly to the quality you produce when they see or hear your name. It's like in acting, the characters Denzel Washington and Chadwick Boseman play in the movies. And for brands like Amazon, Alibaba and Walmart when you think of ordering online from your home, work or your business, those names are embedded in the households of many families.

Become the best in your field

"With confidence, you have won before you have started."
— Marcus Garvey *(Jamaican activist)*

The first thing you should know when you set out to become the best, you must have a purpose for being the best, and it might sound cliché, but your purpose is what makes it more meaningful to the point where you start living it out in small doses, and this can be an eventful experience. If you practice molding your craft every day and try to perfect it to mastery, it will only bring you closer to the goal, rather than wandering aimlessly from it. When you have read through this book and realize that everything in it was given to you for a fundamental purpose, you will then start to design a different you and visualize how it feels to be the best in your field.

There are many stories you can read on becoming the best, but create your own path, it will be very difficult yes, but it will be well worth it. If you are aiming to be a benchmark in your industry, it goes way beyond just doing well; it's making sure you "own" your craft. Think outside of the bubble that everyone else is in; figure out who acts, and who doesn't, because basic thinking produces basic results.

When customers think about the service they need, they should think of you or your company first. Be the standard for which others are measured and do not go so far into ten different things that you can't immerse yourself in one. Find ways to dominate a space and be original in it. How? Well make a list of what your competitors are NOT doing, and do those things, always think of the customers need first. Because if you don't set these goals, there is no way you are going to achieve this. Remember in all things don't compete if you are not prepared yet, because it is wiser to pick your battles in the markets, where you have more advantages over others.

203

Will your work bring forth leaders or followers?

In my years of working for different companies and then building own my businesses, I often sought out the importance of leadership. My earliest example was my mother, even though my father was living in the same house, she did everything I needed see as a wife, a queen, and a lady. My father too was a great man, but he lacked qualities I needed to see as a father, I believe many black men today still lack great leaders around them. Luckily, I turned out better than I expected, all praises to the Most High *God*.

"Excellence is not a singular act, but a habit, you are what you repeatedly do"
— Shaquille O'Neal *(Former professional basketball player).*

I see the quintessence to bring in more young men into leadership roles, but it is more important to have real women in their actual roles as it was originally. This will advance the cultural change we need as a nation of people whether for Blacks, Hispanics, Native Americans, or the other races that are deeply impoverished for true leaders. This means anyone who is in position of power and influence must start from now to identify prospective leaders. And try to mentor them through the difficulties and systematic roadblocks they will face in the early years of their growth to leadership and personal development.

In the book of Titus, chapter 2 of the KJV Bible, it gives guidance on how older women and older men must teach the younger generation on the right path, hopefully they will take heed to this doctrine to live the best life they can possibly live, no matter what status of life they may come from. But truthfully the most enduring and satisfying changes will come from within us, and that is what we must work towards to bring about this cultural change for everyone, so we all can play our respective roles in any community, industry, or areas of our home.

What's the Purpose of Self-Development?

The value everyone must place on self-development should not be neglected as most people think. Some of us either consistently keep brushing off our shortcomings or refuse to face them, while some of us just prefer to be ignorant and mindless out there. The truth is you cannot run from yourself nor from all the things that will come at you in the world. Over time all these unresolved issues and emotions will get bottled up inside and create more encumbrances for your growth.

For any fulfilling result your main focus should be around continuous reading, studying and applying what you have learnt at every stage in your life, and this will allow you to become a better version of yourself every day. The same way learning should never stop, is the same way we must apply the principle to self-development. All of us can start by being more responsible for who we are and what we must do, to better ourselves and the people around us. We all have our roles and this unimaginable potential in us to become anything we desire in this world. And you can do this today or you can do it right now, because we are ones who must make these things happen and not wait for anyone else to come save us or change us.

"People become really quite remarkable when they start thinking that they can do things. When they believe in themselves, they have the first secret of success."
— **Norman Vincent Peale**

Follow up with everything you do

Doing what other people fail to do, will place you in a distinguished position, when there is no one else to follow up or keep track like you. Learn to win the hearts and souls of the people, but DO NOT do it deceitfully or with any unrighteousness.

Sometimes a lot of people don't know how to follow up on assignments that were given out, projects being worked on or even with customers who have regular complaints with their products or services. Don't delay in resolving an issue or a query, act swiftly, but correctly. Don't appear too desperate for a deal, but act enthuse about it, and don't make false assumptions about anything, but ask more questions. These tips will help to you move more prudent in the world without acting pushy or being insensitive. Take mental notes with everyone but always listen keenly.

Chapter 20

Conclusion

In the final thesis of my book, my only hope is that everyone will use these valued lessons to improve their lives and their aspirations to become successful at whatever they desire. But even with all this information it still boils down to the choices you make and if you make those choices in the end. Whether your plans were to get that benchmark status, or to become a successful entrepreneur or professional, no matter what issues may arise to deter your from re

aching that goal, your will power must keep you through all adversities. Sometimes we all want to give up on the journey, but every effort matters to improve you at each breaking point.

Get so confident in your craft that your work will always speak for itself and the value you provide to others will spread across the seas, from this, it will have no boundary nor color. Remember you are in a race to yourself, and you must not watch the competition, only pay attention. The race is not for the swift, but for who can endure, so it doesn't matter if anyone believes in you now, if you believe in yourself first, the real ones will stay, while the others might come around later. When I wrote this book, I wrote it for those who want to find a way out of poverty, out of mental bondage, those entrepreneurs who are struggling, and for people in any profession that are lost and need a different path.

Everyone's path will be different, and every success story will come in an *unusual* way. My good friend Raheim S. Fender who is an author and a teacher said in his book **The Personals... Broken Poetry of Man's Heart,** *"that I most definitely don't consider myself as the best poet, however I do* *feel I have a voice that has an audience,"* and when I read that, it gave me that incentive to put out my work.

Even now if my book only sold a few hundred copies, I would still be happy and be contented, because the numbers wouldn't matter, what would matter is the fact that I published my first book, and I promised myself no matter what happen, I would still do it. Not because I wanted money, but I felt that I owe it to those individuals who wanted to have a voice and the voice for those who wanted a change in their lives.

So, start creating your very own success story by interworking all your challenges, and growth in your journey, setting the standards for how your work will improve the lives of others. I know the time and resources you will spend on developing yourself or the employees in your business should never be wasted; because their personal development and yours can always return a copious reward and this will be a part of your lavish wealth to come.

"There's no shortcut or magic recipe to success"
—Richard Branson *(English businessman)*

Prayers for Success

Scripture of Focus: Preparing for Battle

Exodus 13:17 NIV Bible

[17] God did not lead them on the road through the Philistine country, though that was shorter. For God said, "If they face war, they might change their minds and return to Egypt"

Devotional Message

The scripture says God didn't lead the Israelites on the easiest route to the Promised Land because they were not ready for war. *God* had to toughen them up so they would be prepared for what He had in store. I don't know what religion or belief system you belong to. But don't be discouraged by the troubles that will come because they must come. Trouble is not going to defeat you unless you give in and allow it. It will prepare you and strengthen you for battles ahead. If you trust our *God* in heaven when everything is good, then you must trust Him in times of trouble. Believe, even when you don't understand the disappointment or the circumstances you are going through, it is only TEMPORARY. *God* is directing your steps, most time when you see trouble; there is a greater reward ahead on your journey. If you stay in faith and continue to work you will see the reason why that door was closed, why you miss that big deal or that huge promotion, because *God* has something better in store for you. He already lined up the big opportunities, the healing, and the funding all to move you into your purpose.

LET US PRAY

Heavenly Father, thank you for loving me so much that You are taking all the troubles away that was meant for my downfall, so you can use them for my good. I trust in You Lord to make a way for my success and my prosperity. Even if it seems like I am going backwards, continue to give me the vision and the drive to move forward until my rewards are made known, in Christ name, Amen.

Scripture of Focus: Using your gifts and being your true self
Roman 12:6-8 NKJV

[6] Having then gifts differing according to the grace that is given to us, *let us use them:* if prophecy, *let us prophesy* in proportion to our faith; [7] or ministry, *let us use it* in *our* ministering; he who teaches, in teaching; [8] he who exhorts, in exhortation; he who gives, with liberality; he who leads, with diligence; he who shows mercy, with cheerfulness.

Devotional Message

What *God* has given to us as gifts is an example of what most of us are truly doing and living out today, while some have not found this path yet, it is never too late. *God* urges us to be "light of the world" with our gifts and do his work, but many of us have sacrifice our dreams and purpose for others and have not lived out their true potential. What are you doing with yours today? Is it good or bad? We should allow *God* to work through us to fulfil his purpose on earth, and for which Christ came and sacrifice Himself, so that we may live a better life today. Each one of us has been called to do great works on this earth, whether we can see it now or not, our uniqueness will make us stand out in public or in our homes, so do not suppress your gifts because you do not see your path out, even if you were discouraged by others who lack your specialty and creativeness.

There will always be a demand for your gift and a path for your destination, continue to work at it and never give up.

LET US PRAY

Our Father in Heaven, please help us today to use our gifts and our abilities to teach, to heal and to provide for others who cannot for themselves. Thank you for showing us and changing me into who I am supposed to be and not pretending to be someone else, help others to find their self and not by man standards, but by *Your* standards Heavenly Father. You have created us to be beautiful and a sovereign people, doing wondrous works in *Your* name, please continue to lead us and show us that way, in Christ name – Amen.

Scripture of Focus: Service and Reward for all

Acts 10:34-35 NKJV Bible

[34] Then Peter opened *his* mouth and said: "In truth I perceive that God shows no partiality. [35] But in every nation whoever fears Him and works righteousness is accepted by Him."

Devotional Message

Where the Spirit of the Lord is, there is freedom and when there is freedom there is progress for change and growth. It doesn't matter what your nationality or ethnicity is, your family heritage or your financial status: *God* wants your work to be righteous and true in His eyes and in the eyes of others. He wants you to be free from whatever unnatural, historical, and man-made teachings that has not benefited people and yourself in return. *God* will pour out His abundant blessings and honor on all those who carry out righteous acts, from giving honestly and wholeheartedly to the poor and needy. And performing acts of justice and fairness to others who are treated unjustly.

In Galatians 3:28 it says: *"There is neither Jew nor Greek, slave nor free, male or female, for you are all one in Christ Jesus,"* so *God* is not watching or judging by your race, He is looking at your deeds that is done from your hearts and soul.

Don't let the enemies of deceit and liars in your country or around the world mislead you with religion. Focus on honoring *God's* work of righteousness and watch your blessings increase in every area of your life.

LET US PRAY

Heavenly Father, thank you for leading me onto path of righteousness and accepting my work and purpose regardless of my ethnicity, I choose to do what is right in your sight and honor Your Holy name. Let the Holy Spirit guide me and show me the way, if there is any fault and errors in my life, help me to remove or fix them, so they maybe pleasing to You and others around me. Make me an example of Your goodness all the days of my life in Christ name, Amen.

Scripture of Focus: Facing each day with faith and confidence

Isaiah 43:18 -19 NKJV

[18] "Do not remember the former things, nor consider the things of old. [19] Behold, I will do a new thing, Now it shall spring forth; Shall you not know it?
I will even make a road in the wilderness *And* rivers in the desert.

Devotional Message

As we begin each day, let's start with a heart of thanksgiving and a soul of praise regardless of the circumstances. For a moment just forget the biggest worries and disappointment and don't enter a future dwelling on the past. For there are so many things that we cannot fix or undo humanly because it's out of our reach and limit. Do not let yesterday failures or bad relationships stop you from succeeding or progressing forward. *God* has already prepared a new path for you that will bring you further away from the former things that had hurt you, so He knows your struggle and trials. In Deuteronomy 33:25 KJV it says, "Thy shoes shall be iron and brass; and as thy days, so shall thy strength be." So, believe that *God* will give you strength in each coming day if you trust and believe in Him. You will always have challenges ahead that will cause frustration, sadness, and even death around you. But *God* will see you through it all, because in life these must come.

Fear not, *God* will be your comforter and restore your soul, a lot of people do not know this, but it doesn't matter what religion you're in, or the pass life you had, or the sins you have committed. The biggest sin our father in heaven will not forgive, is us *rejecting* His love and His kindness. So let not your heart be troubled, keep the faith, keep believing and keep praying for your answers and your path will be shown to you in due season.

LET US PRAY

Heavenly Father as we start each day, we confess our needs and our desires to You, that You may grant us according to Your will, lead us out of trials and tribulation each day and give us the strength and wisdom we need to discern what is real from what is fake. Lord *God* we do not know what lies ahead each day, but I know the plans you have for us are for good and to prosper through all season. Let us forget past worries, but not Your works of good in our lives, let our hearts not be troubled when any financial crisis, pandemic or economic downturn arises. We know that you will create path of wealth and peace in our lives, this we pray for and more, in Christ name – Amen.

Scripture of Focus: You can be delivered from all addictions and obsession

1 Corinthians 10:12 -14 KJV

[12] Wherefore let him that thinketh he standeth take heed lest he fall. [13] There hath no temptation taken you but such as is common to man: but God is faithful, who will not suffer you to be tempted above that ye are able; but will with the temptation also make a way to escape, that ye may be able to bear it. [14] Wherefore, my dearly beloved, flee from idolatry.

Devotional Message

If we are not careful our addictions and habits towards many different things can be seen as idolatry, yes, idolatry. Addictions can fall into different categories, but it can be conscious or unconscious, like doing drugs, idolizing the latest fashion wear, gadgets, TV series, even obsessing over cars, your homes, your jobs, your business, watching porn, and stalking people among other things. These addictions and habits can become so dangerous it harms you and other people. It will even block you from living righteously and worshipping *God* first. Whatever you allow yourself to be addicted to, now becomes your master. Matthew 6:24 KJV says, *"No man can serve two masters: for either he will hate the one and love the other; or else he will hold to the one and despise the other. Ye cannot serve God and mammon."* So, we love the things of the world so much that we hate *God's* teachings and cling to mammon representing the idols of the world. Paul wrote, "Don't you know that when you offer yourselves to someone as obedient slaves, you are slaves of the one you obey—whether you are slaves to sin, which leads to death, or to obedience, which leads to righteousness?

Now, if we turn from these addictive habits and NOT let them enslave us, God will intervene on our behalf, when we pray wholeheartedly and ask for help to be delivered. There's no addiction or bad habit that God can't save us from when we turn to Him in *fasting and prayer*.

LET US PRAY

Heavenly Father, I come before you in total surrender to Your *will*, because I am trapped in addictions, bad habits and idolatry, that has influence and caused unhappy moments in my life. I do not mean to indulge in these activities daily, but they have become apart my life and I need Your divine intervention to break these spiritual curses and temptation put before me. Restrict all-demonic access in my life, and protect me from the *evil* ones, so that I am not trapped in their web of deceit and lies. Lead me not into temptation but deliver me from these *entanglements* that weighs me down daily. Father I am asking you to give me strength each moment to "resist" the good feeling over doing what is righteous and true in your sight. Help me *God* to exercise self-discipline and self-control over my life and my habits, so I can defeat all my enemies and immoralities that may come at me daily. And your love and guidance will prevail over me and my loved ones, this I pray, in your Heavenly name – Amen.

Scripture of Focus: Words of Greatness

Psalm 119:105 KJV

105 Thy word is a lamp unto my feet, and a light unto my path.

Devotional Message

Quite often we see potential in other people that they can't see in themselves. When you speak vision into them or show them what they can become, you are helping them to set a new direction into greatness. Our words have power to push people into a divine destiny. I believe that's the reason some people are not living their full potential, because no one has ever spoken faith and confidence into them. Typically, most people will not take the time out to say "hey, your great at this, continue doing it! Or You've got a gift, you're doing some amazing things." I believe that one of our assignments in life is to call out the potential of greatness in other people. Sometimes it can be your calling to help others build a great business, become leaders for change and not be selfish. Always look around for who *God* has placed in your life, they're not there by accident nor coincidence. Take time to study them, see what they're good at, what gifts they have and what they can really excel at? Don't just consider it, go do it and speak visions of greatness over their lives so they know what they can become on their own path. Let your encouragement ignite great works inside, so *God* can guide and lead them to His will and purpose throughout the earth.

LET US PRAY

Heavenly Father, thank you for the great people you have placed in my life. I choose to be faithful, to speak life over them and call forth greatness in them always. Thank you for already bringing me to a newer level even when I can't see it. As we rise higher in wisdom and in wealth, may we never forget *Your* grace nor mercies that *You* extend to us daily, in Christ name - Amen

Scripture of Focus: The true path to success

Matthew 7:7 NKJV

[7] "Ask, and it will be given to you; seek, and you will find; knock, and it will be opened to you. [8] For everyone who asks receives, and he who seeks finds, and to him who knocks it will be opened.

Devotional Message

Most of us have big dreams and great aspirations to become inventors, business owners, political leaders or just the desire to be great in anything. It might seem impossible, but I am reminding you it is not. Everything on earth is humanly possible if we seek it and ask for it. This biblical verse is both spiritual and practical, although many do not believe in the bible and that I can understand. Whatever your heart and mind desires you can attain it, my personal devotion to *God* as always open many doors of opportunity and as allowed me to receive great knowledge and rewards ahead of my time. I know many of us has been toiling very hard for a longtime and no results (Haggai 1:6 KJV). And you might be knocking on doors that still remain close. This does not mean it will come at your timing, it only comes in the season it is ready.

Our endurance with gratefulness given by the father of grace, shows what hard work, perseverance, and patience can do. But many of us give up easily after a few trials and failure.

Our "no" sometimes just means "not yet," and your door is not open yet, but trust in *God's* promises and continue to seek Him and wait patiently until it's your turn.

LET US PRAY

Our Father in heaven thank you for showing us the opportunities that are possible and the path to go searching for it, I chose to keep trusting and enduring the struggles and trails until the doors of opportunity and prosperity will open. Give me patience and humility in your presence, until everything is revealed to me by your will and in your timing, in Christ name - Amen

Love & Light on the journey ahead!

ABOUT THE AUTHOR

Ralton Thompson is an esteemed businessman and a Personal Development Consultant based out of New York City and Atlanta, Georgia. He as years of experience in business and marketing and is a recipient of numerous awards for his work, including the recognition as a top banker for Wells Fargo during his active years. Ralton has worked across multiple industries and is now helping small business owners and young entrepreneurs build broader customer-based products and deliver the best human experience possible. There is no hidden truth that he loves to play life coach and a mentor to younger peers struggling to find their purpose in life.

This is Ralton's first book in a series of work he has written to release in the coming years. Now a full-time entrepreneur, he is transforming readers to become intrepid industry movers and shakers who have inspiring stories that the world needs to hear. His work in a lot of under privileged communities is exceptional for a young leader and is admired by his peers and the younger generation.

Even though Ralton decided to drop out of college to pursue his real-life goals, he still managed to qualify himself with accolades in Management Studies, from the University of the West Indies, Project Management certification through Inter-American Development Bank, and a degree in Environmental Science from Knox Community College just to name a few.

Ralton as dedicated his time and effort in ensuring that everyone succeeds at their desired goals. If you want to connect with his work and his books, visit his website at **www.raltonthompson.com** so can you sign up to receive updates and other upcoming releases.

CPSIA information can be obtained
at www.ICGtesting.com
Printed in the USA
LVHW020039031122
732161LV00014B/841